Book of Orion

Liber Aeternus

Book of Orion

Order of Aset Ka

LUIS MARQUES

Book of Orion - Liber Aeternus

Luis Marques

Occult and artistic concepts by Luis Marques.
Graphics and artwork by Tânia Fonseca.
Revision by Tânia Fonseca and Elizabeth Tray.
Cover design by André Caetano.
Cover photograph by NASA, European Space Agency, M. Robberto and the Hubble Space Telescope Orion Treasury Project Team.

Published and edited in Portugal by Aset Ka

Apartado 52230

4202-803 Porto, Portugal

ASETKA

To contact the author, mail can be sent to the publisher's address using the author's name, as recipient, and the contents will be forwarded. The Aset Ka will not guarantee that every letter written to the author will be answered, but all will be forwarded.

First Edition published in 2012.
ISBN 978-989-95694-2-3

Kemetic Order of Aset Ka
www.asetka.org
public@asetka.org

Book of Orion
Liber Aeternus

Disclaimer

Asetians are by no means harmless beings or the personification of kindness. They do not abide by social standards nor fall under the understanding of the common mind. In the silence and darkness of their inscrutable nature they are known not to be social and often do not nurture an inborn friendliness over society. Their ageless culture is built upon predatory occultism, the dark arts, a powerful layer of spirituality and secrets long forgotten to mankind.

In their dual essence and misunderstood existence, as elemental forces of nature, the Asetians may be gentle, loving and protective, being capable of the most selfless acts of healing and nobility, while also wielding a devastating side that can be fierce, unforgiving and horrifying. However, awareness of this fact does not mean that an Asetian mind is something that you should fearfully run away from. Their legacy echoes a culture that teaches spiritual growth, learning and evolution; that fights stagnation, dishonesty and weakness. They, above all, protect wisdom, shield innocence and enforce loyalty, honor and union. Asetians are the craftsmen of the subtle, the swordsmen of magick and the scholars of arcane wisdom.

But... is it dangerous to study Asetian knowledge?

For the immature and ignorant-minded, the obsessive, compulsive and paranoid; for the weak, the numb and the slow; the ones drowned in a crown of ego or enslaved by a desire of vanity; for those that do not perpetually question the mystical details in life and challenge their own reality; the ones who believe in religion and dogma out of everything that is pushed down their throats; for the disrespectful and arrogant towards everything that they do not know and fear; to all those people... yes, Asetian spirituality is and always will be a very dangerous subject to study and get involved with.

☥

The Order of Aset Ka will not be held responsible for what use is made with the information provided within their work, texts, teachings and practices. The occult science of the Asetians is an expression of the timeless voice of nature that unveils the secret keys to the fabric of immortal consciousness, and as such it is bound to the exercise of responsibility. The potential danger in its misuse is undeniable.

This book was designed for Asetians and the followers of the violet path, but everyone from any walk of life is welcome to read, meditate and question this work. Just keep an open and sharp mind.

Welcome to our world...

Introduction

E m Hotep.

This magickal grimoire is one of the several *Libri* from the Order of Aset Ka used internally as part of its initiatory teachings and occult curriculum.

As the author of the initiatory text, teachings and literary work presented in *Liber Aeternus* - commonly referred as the *Book of Orion* due to the triple nature of its spiritual mysteries - I have been dedicated to the revision and rewrite of my original material, used internally, in order to reflect the paradigm and spiritual formulae for the now flourishing spiritual age - the *Djehuty of the Serpent* - and thereby making it possible for open publication, while still retaining its wisdom and use to any scholar of the Asetian tradition and other students of the mysteries. Although updated in content and form, much initiatory material was included along with secrets on the very nature of spiritual initiation and the unveiling of esoteric keys usually hidden from the seeker without an elevated rank within an occult Order, preserving its potential to other Asetians and to every dedicated occult student. New information was also added in order to aid the initiate with the magickal knowledge he might not possess as well as to provide further study material to those that may not be familiar with some of the most advanced occult concepts being presented within this work, along with the inclusion of images, esoteric schemes and visual artwork created by Tânia Fonseca, including some of her rare hand-drawn pieces of Ancient Egyptian art never before seen in print. The cover artwork of the published book uses an actual image of the Orion Nebula, taken over 500 km above the Earth by the Hubble Space Telescope, and was included in this project with permission from NASA and the European Space Agency. Located over 1300 light years away deep into the galaxy, the nebula found south of the Orion constellation belt is known for its beautiful

✝

violet and red coloration. Such inspiring art from nature lost in the body of Nut is a cradle for the birth of stars. As philosophical as this may sound, the designation is actually quite literal as it represents the closest location of star formation to Earth and has been extensively studied by astronomers - who call it M42 or Messier 42 - providing a wealth of scientific information relating to the formation of the Universe. How revealing that such a timeless symbol of spiritual creation known for having inspired the ancients has now become a provider of answers for both modern scientists as well as contemporary occultists...

The *Djehuty of the Serpent* marks a very important shift in global consciousness but particularly in terms of spiritual awareness and ruling forces for the new spiritual era, as it was outlined in further detail in the published work *Asetian Bible*. It is a time of spiritual liberation, personal growth and inner potential of the subtle over the mundane as the path for balance and understanding. As the *Book of Orion* is my third published work to be released to the general public, its timing and relevance are perfectly in tune with the magickal formulae of the sacred *Three*, explored in depth within this work.

Psychology of Wisdom
As with all my works and teachings, I expect and welcome criticism. Intelligent criticism is a tool that can enhance learning for both the apprentice and the master, while negativism and superficial condemnation is nothing but an effortless demonstration on the power that our culture and influence has to affect and move others, presenting a valuable lesson to the initiate. Five years after the release of the *Asetian Bible* it has become clear the shocking effect that some fields of knowledge and wisdom can have on people, particularly on

weaker minds. The cautious study and observation of such reactions has served as example and learning to many seekers for the past few years and will remain a valuable lesson in history, as while the book became a magickal tool to some and actually changed lives with its violet touch, it also served to bring forth the very best and very worst in people. That alone is a recognizable Asetian signature, present in all forms of Asetian work, art and in the very core of our being. As an elemental force of nature, this path brings forth the devastating truth in people, no matter how painful that may be: without masks, fears or prejudice. It shakes the keystone of their mind to the heart of their spirit, breaking all conditioning and destroying the superfluous, leaving only what is real behind. Many people are afraid to accept reality and have no courage to look into the divine mirror of the Gods to see their own reflection staring back at them. This leads to great imbalance, both mentally and spiritually, which often manifests in lies and dishonesty. It is a form of spiritual enslavement that vehemently opposes growth and self-development. With this in mind I shall now quote a brief paragraph from my introductory text published in the *Asetian Bible*, since its message was not only revealed to be precognitively accurate: it is just as relevant today as it was back then, or even centuries ago.

If someone will criticize our philosophies, beliefs, practices or any other thing related with our own nature, life and metaphysical approach, it is because in some way they feel affected by us. Or else they wouldn't be spending their own energies attacking someone they probably don't even know and that surely would never feel attacked or intimidated by them. So, in this way, and often unconsciously, they are changed by us. We made them move and act just because of what we are and represent. That is our chaotic nature.

The common society will continue to look at us and other occultists as if we are evil incarnate. Many fear what we represent and the things we stand for. As irrational as that fear may be, I believe it is often attached to the manifestation of ignorance. Mankind fears what they don't understand. The words *mystery* and *secret* are often enough to cause discomfort, let alone taking the step into the unknown and having the courage to accept darkness as an evolutionary force of wisdom.

I have always taught the younger and less experienced occult students that hatred, when directed towards them, is one of the greatest forms of flattery and boost to their ego. You can never express hate or move against someone who is not meaningful to you, so those situations are powerful indicators to pinpoint those that you have inspired in life, and who are often unaware on how their negativity is actually expressing a hidden form of admiration and praise. It is an interesting lesson that many have become increasingly familiar with over the years and one that has become particularly clear with the publications from the Aset Ka. Coming from different backgrounds and serving distinct agendas people have expressed opinions against the Asetian culture and beauty, some with respect and nobility while others with pain and anger, making it even a part of their life's crusade. At the same time, others have rejoiced in tremendous praise of our works and legacy, showing that while the reactions to our tradition are so diverse, there is one message that they all bring forth together - the Asetians inspire people to move, create and react. In all forms of expression and manifestation they prove themselves unable to be indifferent to the Aset Ka, never willing to ignore it, and so as a chaotic lesson from nature their spirituality and beliefs are shaken by the violet catalysts that are Asetian art and energy.

As a spiritual force of continuous growth, freedom and empowerment, our elitist message of calmness, balance and dignity remains the same: do not fight or oppose hatred, but instead use it as a lesson to others on your own accomplishments and power, as we have done so often across the ages with our signature indifference and silence. Insult is the ultimate expression of fear and insecurity. It is a clear echo of frustration and the herd mentality, often motivated by rejection. When faced with the wisdom of an evolved mind, haters lose all their power and become mere servants of your own determined will. Unknowingly, they pay you a valuable service. Use them wisely.

"From the deepest desires often come the deadliest hate."
Socrates

My experience as a writer has taught me that the strongest offenses almost invariably come from the ones behind the highest praise. Such vain attacks are usually driven by unstable fans, those you moved and inspired, not by someone that does not care, and are frequently triggered by obsession, rejection and paranoia. That is why I believe that, despite being just emotional food for the ego-centered authors, such forms of criticism and negativity can ultimately be a simple expression of flattery and praise to any accomplished artist. Life is too beautiful, special and brief to be wasted on negativity and ill intentioned people. Break free from the unhealthy influence of those that desire to bring you down to their level and instead rise with class and embrace life to its fullest, valuing every single drop of what it has to offer. Don't take anything for granted, as life is an edification of impermanence. Never surrender to conformism and always fight for what you believe to be fair. Do not fear falling, being judged or making mistakes, as those are the experiences that teach us the very best lessons in life. Remember that you will never be able to please everyone, but most importantly, you don't have to! Simply being true to yourself is already quite an accomplishment where many fail to succeed. Make every day count and celebrate it with joy, no matter what creed, belief system or religion you follow. That is a vital principle of Asetian philosophy, so often underestimated when the focus is not balanced and placed within.

As an occultist and author I have been target of the highest praise as well as the lowest judgment and defamation, as happens with anyone that has created some level of work worthy of reference. While I have always dealt with such occurrences with both indifference and understanding, simply observing how criticism - both positive and negative - unfolds and how the mind reacts to rumor and outside influences, such examination has proven to be an interesting study on the psychology of the human mind. It is quite surprising to verify that most situations develop from people who have an inborn habit of divinizing the ones they admire. Worship and fundamentalist admiration quickly turns into hatred and anger when you are not corresponded. When the mind fears what the heart desires the easier road may manifest by lying to oneself through convincing thought that the object of deepest desire simply does not exist, or that if it does it must have been fabricated to deceive. It is a psychological defense mechanism from a mind that fears experiencing pain, which is a form of self-enslavement.

Some see us like a powerful entity that is beyond reach, which makes no mistakes, sees everything and knows all the answers. This couldn't be further from the truth, as one of the first steps of wisdom is the realization of how little we know and how small we are. I'm no exception. Such situations become even more visible with artists that have struggled to avoid fame and, when dealing with the inevitable public exposure, have chosen instead to embrace a fulfilling private life, such as myself. This happens not only with published authors, but it is common ground with every individual that moves in a field that takes their work to a level that reaches so many different people all over the world. It is inevitable. Someone you deify to a level of obsession is bound to become your greatest demon and personification of evil at some point in time. This is why I tend to discard both the highest praise and the lowest abuse. They are both biased evaluations of your work and merit, and none truly mirrors the factual truth or is the result of fair judgment. If readers, followers or fans would see their admired artists as equals, there would be no obscene praise to the point of ridicule or intentional lies and defamation to the point of absolute vilification. That is because they would see you simply as another soul bound to this realm; that just like them can make mistakes, have qualities and imperfections, and experience good and bad days. We cry. We laugh. We love. Just like you, we will also die someday...

Being a respected author, prominent occult scholar, spiritual teacher, religious leader or any other title that may be brought upon someone - and titles mean absolutely nothing - does not mean that one has all the answers or knows everything. No one does, really. This applies to everyone, from any background and walking any path of life. Learning should always be a never-ending journey; and I can only speak for myself, as I learn something new every single day of my life, often finding the most valuable lessons in the subtler things. Learning is a permanent passion that I intend to nurture until the end of my days.

I know this is one of those messages that sounds profound and people can resonate with, but on the next day get beaten down by their ego and fall into the same traps again. People often close their eyes when the message does not suit their agendas or comply with their expectations. In other words, people try to ignore the inconvenient truths about themselves. Still, the message will remain here, immortalized in paper and ink, for those who are open to change and growth. My work has been through the commitment to honesty by giving people the magickal tools of awareness, which alone do not create their enlightenment, but simply aid in the long road that is their own personal spiritual journey. We may open the doors, but it is always up to the individual whether to sit or to walk.

The students of the Asetian path, as well as occultists from many other serious traditions, are commonly described as rebels, revolutionists and sometimes even insurrectionists. Let me tell you, you must care not for smaller opinions that do not seek understanding before judgment. The path of Asetianism, as a path of the Wise, is not for everyone. If you can feel it within your soul and have a deep desire to embrace it, and if through this culture you can rise to become something greater, then you can only be proud. The world has never nurtured tolerance for beings of deeper thought or for the souls that reach higher. Asetians are the silent scholars unveiling the path of spiritual immortality and the protectors of arcane knowledge. They may rightfully fear you as anyone able to See should be feared, but rest assured that this is not a path of rebellion but simply a path of Truth.

Mysteries of Orion

The term *Sebayt* is an old designation for a very specific form of Ancient Egyptian literature developed in the temples by the hierophants and passed on to the younger initiates as they progressed through the ladders of self development and initiation into the higher mysteries, with a few only accessible to the Pharaoh himself. Scholars believe the word to mean *teachings*, and those documents were seen as true *Books of Life*.

The old Sebayt documents held the mysteries of life and reincarnation through the means of encoded words, an art the priests and priestesses of the ancient temples learned to master in order to keep the sacred information safe. This information was seen as highly valuable, in a time when spirituality and magick held a greater power than that of the physical force found in the armies. Some of these Sebayt are still preserved on papyrus scrolls and are property of modern museums, being for the most part copies of earlier works that got changed, adapted and mutated as mankind evolved and intervened in the spiritual process.

The text we present in this work is not a general Sebayt for the common people, but an *Asetian Sebayt* for the serious occult student that is dedicated to his development and growth through the Asetian mysteries. It is also not a translation of older texts, nor a revamp of ancient religious material, but something written in order to properly reflect the underlying mechanisms of spiritual development that are in tune with the occult formulae from the previous and current *Djehuty*, where the only exception can be found in the contents of the *Book of Sakkara* that contains magickal spells from the *Pyramid Texts*. The Book of Orion presents a complex framework of initiation that takes years to study and lifetimes to master, opening a door to the mysteries of the Universe and to the ever-changing alchemy of Death, Life and Rebirth. Do not expect to see the secrets of life revealed in a simple fashion or a direct manner. Instead, study it only if your commitment to the path of the Elders is strong and determined. If you are seeking quick answers and basic occult literature or magickal recipes, please look elsewhere, as this book wasn't crafted for your mindset. Approach it with no expectations, or its apparent simplicity will deceive and misguide you. It is certainly not a tool for everyone.

The *Book of Orion*, as its name implies, is a triple grimoire. This means that it is comprised of three minor tomes used by the Aset Ka and compiled in a single volume. The three tomes that bring this *Liber* to life are the *Book of Giza*, the *Book of Ipet Resyt* and the *Book of Sakkara*, all of them being distinctive in content and function.

The **Book of Giza** is the core of *Liber Aeternus*, containing the central teachings of this work and the initiatory framework that it can provide. The first book itself is divided into three further sections, as the number *Three* expresses the mystic symbolism and spiritual formulae that it proposes to teach through its initiatory message. Worthy of reference and study is that there are three stars found in the astronomical belt of the Orion constellation that comprises the natural sigil of Orion. This is also expressed in the physical structures erected thousands of years ago in the Giza necropolis, in Egypt, known as *The Pyramids*. These three monuments of Ancient Egyptian origin and timeless power surprisingly reflect the three stars of Orion mirrored above in the night sky. Together they express the central Hermetic teachings from Thoth, often resumed in the passage *"As Above, so Below"* and its mysteries are as profound as they are complex.

The three magickal texts that form the *Book of Giza* are the *Sebayt of Khufu*, the *Sebayt of Khafre* and the *Sebayt of Menkaure*, ancient symbols of the eternal cycle of Death, Life and Rebirth, as well as the major steps of initiation to personal enlightenment. Each Sebayt is composed by thirty-three revelations, further developing on the triple formula of Orion. During its study the initiate will uncover profound lessons on life and the ways of honor that are very much universal and sometimes lacking in humanity, which just like a true Sebayt of the elder days makes this section of the work an actual book of Life and Death for those willing to learn and not to fear. This text is the most cryptic in the whole book and its interpretation should never be approached lightly or literally, as its coded message is both initiatory and revealing. Its study can only prove to be fruitful when done in a spiritual and individual way, with due caution given its subjective nature and the inherent potential for misinterpretation. A first reading is likely to confuse even the most sophisticated student, but after the examination of the following *Libri* included in this grimoire certain keys present in the Sebayt text will slowly start to flourish within the aware mind. The message that can be unveiled within its study is unique and therefore intimate and exclusive to each individual. Rest assured, its hidden wisdom will guide the humble and deceive the selfish. In Asetianism, the three Sebayt can be paralleled with the archetypes from the Lineages of the Asetian Bloodline - Serpent, Scarab and Scorpion, as well as the three separate ways in which subtle energy can be decomposed in metaphysical practice. In terms of Asetian theology, they express the triple nature of Aset - the *Asetian Holy Trinity*.

Under a Kabbalistic perspective, the Sebayt from the *Book of Giza* can be seen as literary expressions associated with the three higher sephiroth in the Tree of Life - Kether, Chokmah and Binah - which are present in the realm of Atziluth, the reality that the Hebrew sages described as the land of emanations and the world of archetypes. They are pure manifestations located above the Abyss of the false sephirah of Da'ath, away from the macrocosmic reality of the manifest world. While approaching this paradigm we have the first realization on how the Kabbalah, as a spiritual technology independent of dogma, can reflect the Asetian mystical system in a very intricate way. As the first sephirah - Kether, meaning Crown in Hebrew - represents the first manifestation of the indefinable veil of Ain Soph, we can see how it resonates with the spiritual essence of Horus as found in Ancient Egyptian myth, the first breath of Aset to be formed. Consequentially, the sephiroth two and three - Chokmah, meaning Wisdom and Binah, meaning Understanding - develop in the Tree of Life as archetypical echoes of the two hidden sisters of Horus, studied in the Asetian tradition as the Primordial Scarab and the Primordial Scorpion; the dual and opposed forces that, when merged, express the foundation of Horus the Elder. These three manifestations that the Hebrew mystics described as the supernal triad, found as the higher sephiroth in the Tree of Life, when united as one single entity express an adequate conceptual representation of the divine veil that is Aset. Following the formation of the Tree of Life through the fragmentation of energy and transmutational process of reincarnation, those three spheres of divine existence have their reflection manifested beneath the gates of the Abyss, as the sephiroth four, five and six - Chesed, Geburah and Tiphareth; Mercy, Strength and Beauty in Hebrew.

If you feel confused by the drawn philosophical connections between the Ancient Egyptian mystery tradition and the Hebrew esoteric system, or if you are new to the study of Kabbalistic mysticism, do not feel overwhelmed by the apparently foreign language used above as those concepts will be explained and developed within the book, particularly in the dissertation on the Tree of Life found in *Liber* יסוד. Such mysteries and subjective occult concepts will be studied in detail and in a progressive manner within the contents of this work while the reader will be taught how to interpret and use the Tree of Life, as well as understand the spiritual wisdom behind such secrets and how they interconnect with the different layers of Kabbalistic thought.

✝

Having said that, it should also be stated that being fluent in the language and wisdom of the Kabbalah is not entirely necessary in order to be able to learn from the *Book of Giza*. This introduction serves to demonstrate the depth and complexity of the knowledge found in its three Sebayt and how universal this gnosis is, reflecting the very nature of spirituality and the fabric of immortal consciousness. So keep that in mind while studying this text, as it was originally developed for students who have undergone some level of initiation and spent a considerable part of their lives studying the mysteries, not only from the Kabbalah but also from countless spiritual traditions of the world and the occult knowledge taught by different mystery schools.

May this also serve as a message, inspiration and incentive, so that when the reader reaches a point of frustration and self-disappointment during the process of growth through this book, he should remember that not only what he is currently studying was created for an advanced level of understanding, as most importantly should be the realization that reaching this far in his studies is already quite an accomplishment, further than the vast majority of people will ever attain. As a student of the occult, the seeker should never forget to question everything and not take knowledge for granted. The occult world is clouded behind a veil of confusion and insecurity, where people often pass their own opinions and interpretations as factual truth; this should be avoided, as while educated debate can be a fruitful tool for the committed student, it may also turn into a sea of misunderstanding when the veil between what is hypothetical and what is true mingles. Being a victim of rumor and falsehood is the fall of an unaware mind, so if your intentions are sincere and your quest for wisdom is genuine, always seek the river that is closer to the source in the mountain, where the water runs free, fresh and pure.

☥

The second magickal document found in *Liber Aeternus* is the **Book of Ipet Resyt** and it incorporates Asetian scripture, an initiatory document with a profound magickal sigil, accurate scientific information on the astrology of Orion, a detailed explanation on the wisdom of the Kabbalah and the formation and use of the Tree of Life, as well as a selection of Asetian poetry of particular spiritual and historical relevance, that together provide important study material for the initiate.

As reference on the nature of this particular book, *Ipet Resyt* are the old words in the Ancient Egyptian language for the Temple of Luxor, where a vital part of this work was written and a place of central significance in the old Asetian Empire in Kemet. It translates to *The Southern Sanctuary* and it was once one of the main Asetian temples that held an important sanctuary to its priesthood.

The first text presented in this second book is *The Touch of Khonsu* and it includes a unique initiatory mantra traditionally only provided to higher initiates of the Asetian path. It is a brief document that is bound to be polemical and raise misunderstanding due to its simplicity. At its core it presents an ancient spell in the secret language of Serkem, as was uttered by Khonsu in the supreme sanctuary of Em-Waset. For those who may not be familiar with the concept, Serkem is a magickal language used within the Asetian temples in the practice of magick, prayer and initiation, being connected with the Ancient Egyptian concept of *Heka*. The name of the language results from the syncretism of two Ancient Egyptian words - Serket and Kem - meaning *Scorpion* and *Black*, respectively. Through its study and meditation each Asetianist is highly advised to avoid the immaturity of falling into its apparently simplistic song and remain aware in order to prevent being deceived by its seemingly benign call.

Following this elemental document we have three distinctive works - *Liber* סוד *יִ*, *Liber Sigillum 333* and *Liber Vox I*, the last one being a compilation of seven poems inspired by Asetian history and mythology.

Liber Sigillum 333 is one of the gems unleashed in this magickal grimoire and provides the reader with the great revelation of *Sigillum 333*; a powerful magickal device developed within the Aset Ka that embodies the full mysteries of Orion in a single sigil, holding within its symbolism a whole world of wisdom. This *Liber* provides an in-depth study of the magickal seal, educating the reader on the full symbolic set being present along with its complex magickal correlations. It also unveils three major initiations in the Orion mysteries, with elements that were held internally in countless esoteric societies throughout history and are now explored in detail. An English translation of the full text was included, along with the original initiatory document in Portuguese, as studied by some of the members from the Order of Aset Ka.

While it is not internal policy to provide such a revealing study in open publication, nor a detailed explanation of initiatory sigils to non-initiated students, we are opening the hidden gates of wisdom in this case, as it is our belief that such information can provide an invaluable resource to our readers in terms of their spiritual growth and magickal understanding. It also serves as a clear echo of our presence in this new era - the *Djehuty of the Serpent* - with its enlightening message of awareness, growth and commitment to truth, which are values nurtured so dearly by all of us at the Aset Ka and ones that humanity must learn to incorporate into their own spiritual path, no matter where their personal road may lead them.

Due to the complex nature of *Sigillum 333* and the potential problems it may present to the occult adept seeking its understanding,

I have decided to include my own *Liber* יסוד in the *Book of Ipet Resyt*, as it is a primer on the wisdom of the Kabbalah that may shed some light on the often subjective concepts of Kabbalistic mysticism, as well as its deep and sometimes surprising associations with our own magickal system you have all learned to recognize in Asetianism. It teaches the major principles of Kabbalistic thought as it develops the magick behind the Hebrew language and how the ancient mystics used this system in order to explain the creation of the Universe. It approaches the formation of the Tree of Life in a clear and structured way, along with several images that visually demonstrate what is being explained in further detail. It explores the multilayered reality of Hebrew mysticism and the many applications of such gnosis, along with its intimate relationship with the Tarot, the universal fragmentation and transmutation of energy, the structure of the different layers of reality and thought, the creation of the Lineages and the initiatory nature of the soul in its quest for enlightenment. If the reader is not fluent in these subjects and intricate branch of the occult, then the study of *Liber* יסוד is highly recommended before venturing into the contents of *Liber Sigillum 333*. These two *Libri* of both Ancient Egyptian and Hebrew inspiration seal the *Book of Ipet Resyt* in glory and power.

It is also important to remind our readers that documents such as *Liber Sigillum 333* are traditionally provided to students after years of study, and are never available prior to initiation, so such information is seeing the light of day in open publication for the first time in history. Despite the potential danger inherent to the release of this kind of knowledge, like the contents examined in the document of *Liber Sigillum 333*, it fills me with a great sense of respect, honor and humility upon the realization that we are sailing through uncharted territory on the vast ocean that is the occult and spirituality, reaching planes of thought and awareness never before accessible out of the most secretive mystery schools of our world. I have no doubt that we are definitely writing history and defining a path that will shape spiritual thought many years from now.

The last work presented in this grimoire is the **Book of Sakkara**, which contains a compilation of ancient religious texts of both historical and spiritual importance. Well studied by Egyptologists and in ancient history circles, most of these texts are known as the *Pyramid Texts* and were found carved in the walls and sarcophagi of the pyramids in Sakkara, Egypt. Modern dating scientific methods discovered that most of these texts are at least over 4000 years in age, making its contents of high importance in terms of Ancient Egyptian theology. This clearly establishes the *Pyramid Texts* as the oldest spiritual and religious texts known to mankind. The most relevant funerary texts are found in the ancient pyramid of the Pharaoh Unas from the Old Kingdom and, unlike the *Coffin Texts*, the *Pyramid Texts* of Sakkara were exclusive to the royal families of earlier dynasties, making them further related to Asetian genealogy and their spiritual teachings. Its contents were later adopted, altered and, in some cases, improved, resulting in the more recent funerary literature known as the *Coffin Texts* and *The Book of Coming Forth by Day*, better known as *The Egyptian Book of the Dead*; all of them notorious for their teachings on the mysteries of Death and immortality, intimately connected with the ancient view on vampirism as maintained in the Aset Ka and its unique predatory spirituality, which is so different from the modern view of the vampire and its superficial side.

In this book, the different funerary and spiritual texts were compiled due to the relevance of each spell to the Asetian tradition and although the vast majority has been translated from the *Pyramid Texts*, I have also included a few utterances from the *Coffin Texts* and *The*

Egyptian Book of the Dead due to their close connection with the kind of magick that this book examines in detail.

Traditional Occultism

It is important to mention that none of the occult documents included in the Book of Orion represent a simplistic manual of any sorts or describe a set of techniques to be used in practice. As stated above, this work is not intended to be a recipe book, nor is the serious occult practice developed in such superficial fashion.

Anyone seeking fantasy or seduced by the populist side of the occult will be deeply disappointed, as this work represents a scholarly study on the esoteric mysteries and the magickal arts approached with maturity, enlightenment and spirituality in mind. It is a book for true occultists, not for lifestylers. Even though advanced esoteric concepts are studied and explained in detail throughout this work, such study should not be approached in a casual way or dealt with in a superficial manner.

The heart of this work lies in the exquisite gnosis from the *Book of Giza* and its practical application in initiation. However, the word *practical* in this case holds a subjective meaning, as the practice itself develops in a personal way through exploration, meditation and magickal work, while the text and its teachings provide a framework for the expansion of consciousness that makes the revealing of secrets possible. How this manifests will be up to the occultist to unveil in his own journey to the Abyss and whether he returns as a conqueror - a ruler of Self and the master of his inner microcosm - or defeated; another formless dot lost in oblivion.

Although seemingly different under a first study, the three major tomes that form this grimoire complement each other in a

✝

profound initiatory way, so do not interpret every section independently at great length, as each holds a specific piece of the greater puzzle. This book is a tool and, as with any other esoteric device worthy of reference, it can be used by the seeker as a door to a fascinating world or, for the most foolish, it can be used against him. Remember that duality is present in every form of true magickal work and that by giving your hand to a creature of light you may end up locked in a cave, just like blindly jumping into a dark ocean may pull you down to the fountain of Truth.

During the study of this book, as with any work from the Aset Ka or another occult Order, it is of relevance to previously understand the significant differences between popular occultism and traditional or classical occultism. I am aware that this remark might not please many interested readers but as I stated above, and in the light of understanding, we must face and accept the inconvenient truths.

Popular occultism refers to the simplistic esoteric culture of common people that is focused on reaction instead of the transformational path of inner growth; the readily accessible and endlessly more superficial side of broad magickal practice. That is the *occult* as seen on television and in other media, as found in the majority of paid workshops and public classes, which is commonly referred to as *Low Magick* in occult circles and is entirely different in content and practice from the occult knowledge and systems developed in the various initiatory societies and found in ancient cultures that have dedicated their efforts to the understanding of nature and serious magickal practice.

Like the name itself implies, popular occultism is most sought after than more traditional magickal systems, being vastly more popular than any serious spiritual path. This is true primarily due to the fact that people often prefer what is easy, avoiding the longer and more dangerous roads, which are in fact the ones that are able to teach them the valuable lessons in life. It's the common mindset of superficiality and vanity, endlessly obsessed with the physical and the mundane, unable to grasp into the subtle aspects of their own existence; the trap of instant gratification, that like a drug enslaves the mind with what it can immediately achieve, blinding the eyes - otherwise naturally curious and created to learn, seek and grow - into mere devices of futility.

On the other side of the vibrational scale there is traditional occultism, often referred to as *High Magick* and the *Great Work* by the mystery schools. It refers to a diverse set of practices, hidden wisdom and initiatory information that is developed and used in honor, respect and exclusively for the spiritual evolution of the initiate through the means of an expanded understanding of the Universe and the mysteries found in Life and Death. It is a field of gnosis achieved through dedicated study, initiation and responsible practice that differs greatly from anything at the reach of popular occultists, commercial psychics and fortune tellers alike, by the simple fact that it is *secret.*

In this case, the word *secrecy* holds a deceptive connotation. Occult wisdom isn't secret by any desire for status, elitist mindset or to fulfill a hungry ego. It is secret to empower and maintain a much greater cause, which is related with how much power lies behind the doors of initiation that every student must open to look right into the *Eye of Darkness* and fall into the *Well of Wisdom.* Power draws responsibility and only when a high level of spiritual maturity is attained that same power can be wielded and properly mastered. That is the natural and universal elitism of occult practice, one that is so often misunderstood, in particular by those that do not have access to such gnosis.

The whole paraphernalia of superficial occultism that floods modern society by the means of poorly researched documentaries, dishonest commercial books, sinister magazines, misleading workshops and artist wannabes serve as a cloak of ignorance to protect and ensure the privacy of real life occultists. The truly initiated do not appear on television to exploit their practices, rarely accept invitations to give self-promoting interviews about their craft and, most of all, keep their knowledge, power and life private.

Insecurity and low self-esteem has moved many confused people into a desperate quest for cheap fame and exposure unrivaled in any other time in history, where the focus on outside influence and the voice of ego led to a complete loss of the sense of Self and respect. Only the wise can truly value the meaning of privacy, as they have already conquered themselves, hence not being ruled by the image others may have of them. In other words, they are free.

> *"He who controls others may be powerful but he who has mastered himself is mightier still."*
>
> Lao Tzu

Personally, I could never understand the seductive appeal many seem to find in notoriety and praise, probably because I cannot truly value a legacy that receives no criticism, as that would only imply a work that challenges absolutely nothing, being ultimately useless. I always invite criticism - the good, the bad and the ugly - for all the possible reasons that I am known to defend and teach. It is my belief that fame as a form of outside recognition is in no way an indicator of personal success, as that is defined by inner balance and growth. If you need the praise and recognition of others to feel accomplished then you are not really free, as true happiness can only come from within and that needs no outside approval. The way each individual sets his personal definition of success marks the determinant difference between a mind that focuses on the outside - being guided by the image and opinion that others develop of them; a slave of vanity - and one that focuses on what is found within, being free of the conceited conditioning of ego.

It would be foolish to assume anything different, as spiritual accomplishment enlightens the individual with a level of freedom whereby he experiences no need to prove himself or any other manifestation driven by the lack of confidence in Self. That is an essential layer of the inner work developed by the students of traditional occultism and an esoteric field that Orders such as the Aset Ka study, protect and develop in such a serious and mature form. That is the path treaded in Asetianism and followed by the nameless ones who freely but strongly dedicate themselves to the timeless quest of spiritual evolution through such a hard and mysterious road.

So often misunderstood and misrepresented in the modern world, Asetianism is not a religion but a cultural and philosophical legacy that reflects a way of life maintained through inner growth and a profound spiritual path. Many feel threatened by our elitist stance and so-called arrogance while their own society grows on a foundation of betrayal, selfishness, falsehood and the glorification of the most superficial of values; mankind strives on the perpetuation of false morality while it fails to understand the very core of Asetian thought like the meaning of honor, loyalty, trust, unity and love. People abuse such words, overusing them with empty meaning as a shallow reflection of their desires and expectations, yet they all represent so much more than just meaningful words.

While studying the mind and its intimate relation with spirituality it is of particular interest to observe that, for the most part, the ones seeking Asetianism out of genuine passion for the quest to find themselves, to understand nature and to develop a clearer understanding of life are the students that find in this tradition the transformational properties and wisdom to enlighten their path, in whatever way they chose to embrace it, learning valuable lessons that they will hold unto until the end of their life.

On the other hand, the ones seeking the Aset Ka and its teachings due to its distinctive mysterious allure and moved by the idea of power, superiority and fantasy are ultimately driven away in the mist of confusion and disappointment as a result of their own self-deceptive expectation. The Universe teaches in the most mysterious ways, so often the humble can find answers where the egotistic can only see a useless rock. They may look up to the stars and not see their movement, assuming they are lifeless and static in their limited vision. When motivation is not placed in the honesty of the heart, inspiration will not find the right key for your happiness.

When we state that the path and teachings from Aset Ka are not for everyone, in no way does that imply some sort of discrimination expressed in any form. Instead, it is a simple assessment of the factual truth that not everyone is ready for the level of awareness, honor and dedication that it takes to reach understanding through our tradition. The gnosis of the Asetian path knows no gender, race or age - it is Universal.

Asetian philosophy has always been a beacon of hope in an unbalanced world that fears its very own weakness, instead of acknowledging it in order to seek the key to overcome it. The violet legacy, as a powerful hymn of freedom, has always opposed those that seek to impose limitations and barriers within spirituality and mysticism; those who seek to severe, manipulate and distort the natural bond that every being has with the many layers of divinity. In this unconditional freedom, which an adept experiences by getting rid of all forms of limitation and expectation, it is vital to nurture inner focus and awareness to prevent falling into the traps of ego and delusion, often manifested in the superficial population by the embrace of a deluded life of fiction, masks and role-play that in no way represent the profound reality of occult science, spirituality, esoteric art and, most importantly, the eternal foundation of the Asetian culture.

From a scholarly perspective and unlike the aim and scope of other occult and religious paths, Asetianism is a tradition, discipline and way of life that balances and unifies the fields of science, spirituality, magick and art. The Aset Ka stands as a banner against the raising of limitations in spirituality and the sacredness found within, but also manifests as a true adversary for those that limit themselves and others when driven by their failures, insecurities and handicaps. It challenges every subtle detail that may hinder or interfere with the attaining of full potential buried in Self, and for that the Order has become increasingly inconvenient to the narcissistic minds and within many circles.

The Art of the Ancients
I want to take the chance to openly thank Tânia Fonseca from the Order of Aset Ka, for again taking the time out of her busy life and spiritual practice to dedicate her energy to another major project and for providing unquestionable support and insight through this venture to bring out to the public something that wouldn't normally be at their reach if it wasn't for the passion, inspiration and art of such evolved beings as herself. The dignity she has always shown in her

life, work and art deserve this honorable mention, as it has been a humbling experience to teach and learn alongside such a beautiful soul.

Albeit misunderstood by the less aware, my path has been though the embracing of the inspirational science, magick and art of Words.

The power of words, not only through the means of language but also manifested by the realm of symbol and sigil, has been a personal form of magick and spirituality that I have embraced for many years, as well as developed and explored into the deepest dungeons of thought. With its roots in the forgotten culture of Ancient Egypt, where it was known as *Heka* and made legendary by the scholars, priests and Pharaohs; we call it the *Art of the Ancients*, or the *Touch of the Elders*, and you may have seen and felt glimpses of its flame through my literary works.

As surprisingly as it may appear at first glance, without words the human being is not capable of conscious thought. The mind and body have the ability to feel, but without language, there is no intellectual thought. Feelings are manifested energy, so they exist in the realm of purity, in the land of subtlety. Thoughts are words embedded with meaning, so they exist in the realm of magick. I hope that through my work the students of the occult, spirituality and the mysteries may come to respect and value what we consider to be one of the oldest and most powerful forms of art, magick and wisdom.

The magick and power hidden within this book should be cherished and honored, as it will only respect those who approach it with a pure heart and a loyal soul. Not only because when a writer produces a work of spiritual value those words are eternal, permeating the inner consciousness of those it touches for all eternity, as it is also in this case a work resulting from the everlasting gnosis of the Ancient Egyptian mysteries, with its beauty and esoteric symbolism hidden beneath the immortal power of written Word.

> *"The aim of art is to represent not the outward appearance of things, but their inward significance."*
>
> Aristoteles

We are definitely living in an exciting era, and the potential presented in some of the teachings revealed within the following pages of this book is immeasurable.

This work is dedicated to self-development and the transformational opportunity of spiritual growth, as it expresses layers of wisdom that have not only been intimate, but also truly transcending and enlightening to me over the years. They manifest my profound belief that the states of awareness and understanding can only be attained when you look within and learn to ignore the distracting noise of the mundane. It teaches you to trust yourself and by that to conquer yourself in the process. I am certain that much of what is exposed through this work will not be properly understood, as that is inevitable due to the very nature of such occult teachings, but approach these pages with joy and without prejudice, so you shall find the warmth of the flame within. It is unequivocally the result of an act of love.

The message presented within this book to every hungry seeker is that of a mindful observation of nature, as the mysteries are unveiled all around us and presented through the most subtle things as true gifts from the Universe; to avoid the perpetual trap of converging your focus and efforts in the tangible reality of the mundane, but instead to

✝

commit wholeheartedly to the study and pursue of your inner and higher realities by a permanent process of learning through every form of knowledge, presented in any shape, aspect or manifestation and independent of cultural weight and ancestry.

There is no true mastery without embracing life as an eternal student, for a spiritual master must first and foremost be a seeker as well as a teacher. In fact, the unusual length of this introductory text and the depth of the message it carries make this document alone a valuable resource and compass to the students of the occult. Lessons are unveiled in many forms and in the most unexpected ways, so nothing should be underestimated, for some of the most enlightening teachings are sometimes taught through silence.

For the victims of an unbalanced ego or to anyone suffering from delusions of grandeur, simply look up in a clear night and gaze into the vast ocean of stars; it will show you the insignificance of us all. It is a simple lesson that always puts life back into perspective when our mind goes astray. A sincere advice to all my readers is to study this work not only once, but many times, as with every new reading you will uncover greater mysteries, all leading up in the mystical ladder of initiation towards the greater mystery of all - yourself.

Read the pages within this book carefully and tread its teachings with strength and courage. Do it at your own risk…

May the Ka be with your Ba.

Luis Marques
Order of Aset Ka
2012

Asetian Manifesto

To become an Asetian is to die and be reborn.

To forget all you have learned and learn all you have forgotten.

To be an Asetian is to be blessed with everlasting Love.

Is to be cursed by a never-ending thirst for perfection.

An Asetian is a fierce warrior, a faithful lover and an eternal concubine. Having the power of the Pharaoh, the discipline of the Samurai, the knowledge of the Wizard and the commitment of the Geisha.

Kemet is our Holy Land. The genesis of our immortal Ba.

The Tao is Knowledge. Power is through Blood.

Our Ka is sacred.

Our essence is the storm raindrops in the ocean of mankind, the winds that blow on their faces and the quakes that shake the very foundations of their ground.

We are the children of the Gods.
We are the Cursed Ones and the Blessed Ones.

We live in Secret. We live in Silence. And we live Forever...

Book of Giza

And they are Three.
Eternally reflected in the sky as Orion,
gazing at the golden desert.

Sebayt of Khufu

Awakening to immortality

† Death †

Mighty Uraeus that crowns our path
Your mysteries remain behind the timeless veil
At the hand of your Art our magick flies forth
Rising within hides a cradle to the Gods

ζ

1. May the Serpent kiss the infinite of Her cold beauty.
Her gift was eternity and everlastingness.

2. Magick is the fine art of crafting the invisible.

3. Behind the immortal gaze lies a poison that even Gods shall fear.

4. Storm the abyss with all thy power and never rest but at the feet of circular perfection!

5. The fingerprint of our essence is enthralled in memories and sealed deep within their forbidden desires.

6. We are not the engine, nor are we the wheel.
We are the ones that choose its direction.

7. When fully united, without ego or weakness, we become the greatest invisible force this world has ever witnessed.

8. The ensemble of the Gods floats in the cosmic dust of immortal consciousness.

☥

9. Ankh. Khepri. Ka. Tiet. Was. Ba. Ib.

These are the forces that command the Universe.

These are the keys that open the Ways.

These are the tools that hold the Secrets.

10. The purest personification of art is under the mastery of magick.

Manifestation is through Word.

Flame is through Love.

Understanding is through Wisdom.

Honor and respect the Art of all arts!

11. Only in the most arid of deserts can you find the purest water.

12. Thy beast lives within!

Unleash the lion so that it can feast on the thoughts of your enemies.

Their laugh is the sound of fear when crying on the prejudice of thy nature.

13. Fight not to win. Fight to make a stand.

Determination is the key to awareness.

Hunt not to feed. Hunt to learn.

Knowledge is the key to shape the world.

Destroy not to kill. Destroy to transform.

Evolution is the key to immortality.

✝

14. What fools despair to conquer the wise struggle to avoid.

15. Gods feast in the night that equals the day as the wind blows from cold to flame. So the wheel starts to rotate.

16. Smoke rises from the mountain of wisdom. Danger is eminent!
Focus your senses and gather your awareness. Do not vacillate!
Haunted in lost despair their dreams remain.
Only then, I shall become the dreamcatcher.

17. Hell rises and falls but heaven belongs to the inscrutable dreams of the darkest mind.

18. Become the fallen. Be the opposer. Let the adversary manifest...

19. Darkness is Light but there is no flame inside the white dawn.

20. True strength can only be measured in the ethereal fabric of the soul. All else is irrelevant!

21. May the blood from the black Sun rise high in the skies of the condemned abyss. Fear me not! There is no wisdom in fearing what is beyond your control. We are living Falcons, the damned blood of Her prince.

☥

22. The veil can only cover our light from the eyes of mortals, for the ancients can see past any spell.

23. The timeless dance of inner truth can only be perceived in the absence of movement.

24. May oceans of fire consume the essence of our weakened preys.

25. Give me Your strength to defend in crises;

Your wisdom to master in need;

Your wings when loosing balance;

And Your poison to serve cold on our enemies' favorite table.

26. Whispers are elephant footprints in the steps of giants.

27. If the hawk lifts you up in the battlefield, feed him.

28. The breath of the Dragon is lethal.

That is why you should be the one commanding it.

29. Your voice alone can make a lot of noise.

Your voice inside a crowd cannot be heard at all.

An Asetian never tries to talk louder than the surrounding crowd.

An Asetian becomes that crowd.

30. Water is a gifted essence;

A realm of consciousness in the ether.

Always cleanse with the blood of the Gods!

31. I shall become the lion, the hawk and the serpent.

Just like the infinite and the zero are one and the same, eternity hides in the birth from the cosmical virgin.

32. For he shall rise mightiest among the living, as Wadjet biting poisonously and vigorously. He is the one that Lived and the one that shall Return; the crownless king of the silent Empire.

33. Beings of Immortal Flame.

They were born to conquer and tame.

Ancient rulers of all their kin.

Forgotten wisdom is still their reign.

The secret language from the Pharaohs of Kemet!

☥

Sebayt of Khafre

Journey through the halls of despair

† Life †

Forces of chaos; light of the living
The ones that stand between the ways
You raise the Ba to the height of Nut
In times of darkness you fade away

ε

1. The Universe is our chosen realm. Energy is our tool.

May the world bend and adapt to our own inner microcosm.

2. Don't haste your powers into the depths of oblivion.

Laugh at thyself! Manifest the Fool in the Zero!

No force will hold sway over you again.

3. Love is an ally but also a deception chest.

Open it with caution and remember that pleasure is also pain.

4. Be loved. Be praised. And be consumed.

5. Let the Flame be your warmth and guidance in the times of need.

Let the Fire illuminate the ways in the age of darkness.

6. The ancients studied the wisdom of Djehuty.

Later to be described in the mysteries as Thoth.

Remembered by the Greeks that called him Hermes.

But only at night his True Name can be seen.

"As Above, so Below."

He uttered and sealed the Law in the beryl.

☦

7. The firm paws of Anubis can be seen by your side when the Ba goes forth. His dark shadow remains in your presence.

Father of Silence. Children of Death.

Eternally keeping the protective watch...

8. Smile at the loud! Ignore the false rulers and their weaknesses!

Never fear who screams in the clear. Their vulnerabilities are wide and open. The greatest danger comes silently and swiftly, moving like a poisonous snake.

9. Oh young children of Nun so unaware you have become.

By ignorance you prosper in your little world of delusional nullity.

10. The cloak of despair enchants the mundane.

Lift it and see above or cover within and plunge below.

11. The laws of the Ba can be found in the sky of the desert when reaching the night that Thoth has chosen to sleep.

12. Bow down to your Master! Break down your Ego!

Both of them can send your Ba into oblivion.

13. Celebrate in their honor and bring a flame before Her presence, for Her beauty carries the Light of all lights.

14. He who does not cherish life does not deserve to be among the living.

15. No act is as pure violence as the power of His hidden Word.

16. Do not feed the wolves before watching them run in front of your shadow.

17. Manifestation is through the ether.

Invoke the wisdom unto thee.

Call their name upon the altar of intoxicating night.

18. Mortals shall serve the darkness they failed to cherish.

The ones seeking power through our mythical flame shall only find illusion and inner pain.

19. The key lies in the mouth of the beast that died for her wicked master!

20. The Voice and the Flame can sing the same tune when you perform the ultimate sacrifice.

21. Only a true assassin can see past the gate with two-headed goats.

Destroy him, break him and kill him, or he will consume you.

The monster lives inside you.

22. Bask in the light of all abominations for only when going through the gates of the abyss you shall find your answer.

23. Do not pretend to be elite. Become elite.

Do not pretend to fly above. Rise above.

The fools watch as the wise conquer.

They condemn as we feast in silence.

Our rule is their song of despair.

The hidden cloak beneath their nightmares.

24. The eyes cannot be trusted for their tale is that of deception.

To see their reflection you must sacrifice your awareness in the song of perfect trust…

25. Wise are those who can find patterns in the chaos. But be wary as the path to such gnosis is guarded by a three-headed daemon.

26. The most dangerous power is the one you nurture in secret, manifesting its apotheosis only when no soul can believe in its existence.

27. Weakness hides in the mind of those that cannot See.

Overconfidence is the pit of the Fallen.

Acknowledge your own ignorance or die in vain for the ego projects a distorted mask of your inner Truth.

28. It is safer to face a strong enemy in the field of battle than to fight a war by the side of a weak friend.

29. Look above, but do not fear, for through the abyss we have fallen and back to it we shall return.

30. Behold the gates of condemnation!

Can you speak their language in reverse?

31. Do not feed from the weak. Feed from the ancient.

But be ready to be preyed upon.

32. In the inner throne lies the seed of all vices for the temple of purity hides in another door and the cosmos is written in reverse.

33. Beings of Eternal Change.

Fluid voices between the realms.

Mirrored echoes of the crown.

Lost awareness in a sea of living.

The secret language from the Priestesses of Kemet!

☦

Sebayt of Menkaure

Descent to the Duat

☥ Rebirth ☥

Vultures of shadow in forbidden beauty
You leave all mortals enthralled in awe
Disguised as silence you master your poison
The strength of the Mother is your hidden cue

δ

1. Loyalty is a sacred jewel protected by the Gods.

A mystical gem held when the divine knows no doubt.

I give my Ka to Her purpose, as my essence is forever Hers.

2. The Ancients may sleep, but be warned: they will always wake up.

3. They were only Three.

Yet, they moved a nation.

They were only Seven.

Yet, they conquered the desert.

They became endless.

Yet, they were forgotten.

They became legend.

Then, they were remembered.

4. Condemn thought! Condemn action!

Sharpen your senses for they are coming…

5. The flow of time never stops.

It is the cryptic cycle of Death, Life and Rebirth.

Can you see the reflection from the triple path in the endless river?

☥

6. One reign shall fall and another begin.

The wheel shall rotate, endlessly.

Overcome yourself and Become.

7. Unconditional loyalty to the Royal Serpent!

8. I shall rise above all mortals with the wicked powers of death.

Find my Name at the reign of silence in the seventh day.

9. Fear the devastating Dark Flame.

That means to fear yourself above any other!

10. The longest journeys cannot be measured in the length of mortals but in the depth of the inner realm.

11. The mountain of wisdom is never reached by those who profess lies of the sacred past.

12. Energy and Love ignite the alchemy of the Soul.

13. If they say no thou shall be able to see the lie in their tongue and spill terror before their names.

✝

14. Perfection is subtle.

Subtle is not perfection.

Simplicity is a process, not an end.

15. In darkness lies a mystery that has the power to shine brighter than true light.

16. Forgiveness is not for the worms of disloyalty.

Pity them not! Pity is for the weak.

Trust is not for those unable to conquer it.

Blame them not! Blame is when you care.

Power is not for those unable to respect it.

Curse them not! Curses are for enemies.

Now, you stand Above.

17. The divine glimmer of the Amethyst can fade; the body, broken into pieces. But its ethereal purity remains untouched since the time of the Elders.

19. Her name was concealed and Her legacy forbidden.

Touching Her soul is the sin of the Gods!

20. From the light of thy eyes resonates the depth of sexual abyss.

Hidden memories. Hidden secrets. Hidden pleasures.

☩

21. Oh mighty daemons of the ancient world:

Rejoice in darkness and flame.

Never in shame, toast to your victory!

In silence you guide. In secret you protect. In honor you demand.

Oh, my love, ahead gleam the thrones of the immortal Gods!

22. There are seven Keys, but they manifest through twenty-two initiations, sixteen entities and forty signs. To bring them to life you need the steady hand of the artist and the womb from an act of Love.

23. Before striking blindly always look within.

24. The Sting of the Royal Scorpion pierces beyond blood and flesh.

25. Holy Aset, Goddess of all Gods.

Violet Lady of the Flame.

Eternal Mother of the Asetians.

Genesis of our immortal Ba.

Prey upon our enemies.

Vindicate our honor.

Cleanse thy sacred Name!

26. All nature is triple. The One that becomes Three.

Birth comes in the form of One, Two and Three.

27. Truth is an ethereal pond hidden among the stars.

28. Oh Serket you wield the terrible voice of despair!

Remember her name but fear her flame.

For only through the grip of her sword few fought as many.

By her inscrutable scream the small became tall.

So the few were seen casting a shadow above the many.

29. At the end of time we shall ride together as one...

For Bast, the princess that shielded a nation!

For Neith, the arrow that enslaved the desert!

For Serket, the flame that burnt immortals!

Together they rule the three legions of eternal despair.

30. May the strongest of Flames flourish from within the Sacred Women and burn all thy race down to a forgotten reign!

31. Lustful is the Woman.

Oh warrior princess of Thebes.

Your enemies fall under your whispers.

By covering the Sun with your immortal arrows shall Seth fight blindly in the cold!

✝

32. The Scorpion Stings.

The Scorpion Cries.

The Scorpion Dies.

33. Beings of Sexual Flame.

Wielders of immortal honor.

Scholars of the most mysterious silence.

Humble protectors of the One.

The secret language from the Warriors of Kemet!

✝

This is where we stood at the dawn of the ages.

All paths led us to this very same road.

And so it begins...

Note

During study and ritual any reference to the text should be done through the following syntax:

Liber Aeternus Sebayt.Utterance

Example: *Liber Aeternus* II.22

This reference would point the initiate to utterance twenty-two in the Sebayt of Khafre, where the following text can be found.

> *"Bask in the light of all abominations for only when going through the gates of the abyss you shall find your answer."*

Book of Ipet Resyt

My army is the thunder in the sky and the beasts from the earth, the wind in the air and the tides of the sea.
My army is Me.

✝

The Touch of Khonsu

Oh mightiest Prince of the Nefer
The winds cry for you in Em-Waset
Our land burns in furious pain
As the desert storms in the agony of your absence
For your name is still our Reign

Har Khun Ka

Shen Te Num

Ka Khba Khonsu

Ankh Ba Khunsu

Har Khun Ka

Shen Te Num

Ka Khba Khonsu

Ankh Ba Khunsu

Har Khun Ka

Shen Te Num

Ka Khba Khonsu

Ankh Ba Khunsu

☥

Har Khun Ka

Shen Te Nun

Ka Khba Khonsu

Ankh Ba Khunsu

Har Khun Ka

Shen Te Nun

Ka Khba Khonsu

Ankh Ba Khunsu

Har Khun Ka

Shen Te Nun

Ka Khba Khonsu

Ankh Ba Khunsu

Framework

Initiatory spell uttered by Khonsu in the supreme sanctuary of Em-Waset.

Note

The opus matter of this initiatory document, although brief and simple in appearance, brings within its energies a profound magickal utterance that until now has only been available to trustworthy students within the Aset Ka due to its power and spiritual significance. For this reason it is presented here without foreword, guidelines or initiatory procedure, maintaining its powerful magickal key hidden in the Duat.

Without proper training and the aid of wisdom caution is advised when exploring the magick presented through these words. Responsibility is a requirement of wisdom, and respect, a condition of evolution. Without them, the vault of beauty provided within this sacred text shall never be opened.

For only those who seek selflessly and loyally shall See...

Liber יסוד

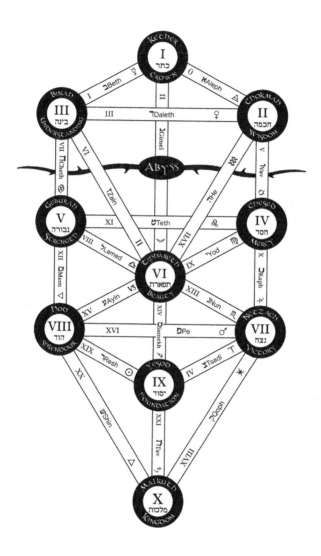

Since the elder days the Asetians have been passionately dedicated to the study, development, perfecting and protection of a multitude of mysteries, schools of thought and knowledge, from science to the most intricate occult arts, developing from all corners of the world throughout different cultures. Among such a vast ocean of wisdom the Asetian Eye has been focused on the hidden spiritual layers of nature that hold the power to reflect the keys to the mysteries able to unveil reality in its purest form.

*T*he sages of old set forth on a quest to attain the unattainable: to comprehend the incomprehensible nature of divinity, and by that to understand themselves. Through the means of meditation, magick and science, along with the selfless observation of nature and the recurring elements found in the chaos, they came to several spiritual and philosophical realizations. That knowledge is what we know today as the Kabbalah – קַבָּלָה.

Developed by Hebrew mystics, the Kabbalah is a powerful spiritual technology that, while mirroring the reality of the cosmos and the essence of the inner Self, with all its layers, complexities and dynamism, can be applied to a variety of esoteric fields without the need of proper religious dogma. In essence, the teachings of the Kabbalah define a framework to understand reality.

It is out of the scope of this document to study the possible origins of the Kabbalah, as its roots are still shrouded in mystery and doubt to contemporary historians. As scholars of the Asetian culture we could theorize that the Jews who abandoned Egypt left with more than just food and wooden staffs. They left from a land that was, and still is, known for its immeasurable spiritual knowledge and mystical power.

Traditional Jewish thinkers profess that the origin of the teachings found in the Kabbalah dates back to *Eden*, a mythological place described in the *Book of Genesis* where the first man and woman lived after being created by the hands of God. In other words, it represents a conceptual era at the dawn of time, much akin to the Egyptian timeframe most Asetianists have come to know as the *Sep Tepy*. Speculation aside, most scholars agree that Kabbalistic knowledge predates Christianity by at least several centuries, but tracing it further back might be hard due to the teachings and initiations being traditionally passed down by word of mouth only to a select few and to the very secretive nature of this kind of mystical thought.

The Hebrew rabbis often state that the original teachings of the Kabbalah were obtained in ancient times from enlightened beings that were not human. Through their own mind, cultural background and the lack of proper understanding they described them as *angels*; wise creatures, owners of mystical wisdom and philosophical secrets, at a time of great spiritual and religious influence of the Ancient Egyptian empire. Who were these mysterious *angels* that held the magick and wisdom that men called Kabbalah, something they saw as so powerful that they only dared to unveil its secrets to a small elite? The answer to such a question and the hidden keys to all its implications may be long lost and forgotten, but one thing remains certain, as with all other forms of knowledge and culture humans have distorted and changed this ancient wisdom to suit their own needs, ideals and fears...

From an Asetian scholarly context it is relevant to state that although parts of the wisdom explored within this *Liber* have originated in Egypt, the historical fact is that we are exploring elements of Hebrew origin and mystical concepts that have their major development in the culture of old Israel. Some of the interpretations found in this book are the result of intensive study on Kabbalistic wisdom and personal research, experience and practice, being related with the Ancient Egyptian spiritual mysteries as studied in the Asetian tradition of the Aset Ka, with a focus on the initiatory secrets and occult wisdom found hidden in the Kabbalah. The seeker interested in the classical religious side of the Kabbalah as studied in traditional Judaism will find the fundamentals of this doctrine in the older texts, originally in Aramaic and Hebrew, as the *Zohar* and the *Sepher Yetzirah*.

This further attests to the learning approach developed within the Aset Ka, that as an initiatory Order of mysteries has inspired the exploration of every form of spirituality developed in history along with the unbiased understanding of many cultures of the world, independently of historical significance in terms of politics, wealth, influence and prosperity. To a learned Asetianist it also serves as an expression of the universal nature of the Asetian tradition and how a deeper exploration of its many aspects can also aid in the learning of different beliefs, religions and cultures.

The Violet lips truly speak the voice of Understanding.

Every time that I am asked to teach about the Kabbalah from a spiritual non-religious perspective, one of the questions that I get asked most often from other occultists who are new to the Hebrew mystical system is why there are so many different spellings for the word *Kabbalah* and what do all those differences mean.

There are several differences, particularly on the level of an introduced coating of dogma and how they interpret the divine, but at a core level they all pretty much have the same foundation.

Kabbalah is the original transliteration of the Hebrew word meaning *receiving* and it is related with the mystical traditions that are found in early Judaism. The meaning behind the word *receiving* is due to its original secretive nature, where it was only passed down from master to apprentice as an oral tradition. In its traditional format you could not simply decide to go learn about the Kabbalah or become an educated Kabbalist student, as you would have to earn it in order to *receive* it.

Quite simply, this designation and concept refers to an initiatory form of wisdom that could only be passed down from a learned and experienced teacher, rather than being openly accessible to someone randomly seeking it.

All the other spellings and variations of the name refer to adaptations of the Kabbalah that have been developed from the original Hebrew system. For example, due to the lack of a proper mystical layer in their own tradition, some Christian sects have adapted this wisdom and called it Cabala, while the Hermetics use it extensively in the many systems of Western mysticism and ceremonial magick but spell it Qabalah.

In Asetianism we usually maintain the original spelling of *Kabbalah* as it better defines the purity and background of the traditional teachings, but hold no particular rules if someone prefers to use one of the alternatives. Due to our intimate and inseparable relation with Ancient Egyptian culture, some occultists have identified our approach to the Kabbalah as a flavor of Hermetic Qabalah, since the Greek wisdom of Hermes Trismegistus, which gave birth to Hermeticism at the heart of the Western mystery tradition, is merely an expression of much older gnosis developed by Thoth in Egypt. This connection is not necessarily inaccurate, but due to the specific nature, esoteric symbolism and wisdom of all forms of Asetian knowledge, magick and culture, other versed occultists refer to our approach to Hebrew mysticism simply as *Asetian Kabbalah.*

This document is intended to work as a primer on the study of the Kabbalah and the ancient wisdom of Israel from an Asetian perspective. It provides the basics - the *foundation* - to understand this esoteric system and its major elements in an unbiased and non dogmatic way, while at the same time providing the spiritual and mental tools to develop a deeper understanding under an Asetian mindset and its hidden potential to be explored in magickal practice. It is important to understand that this text was designed specifically for students of Asetian Kabbalah, where some interpretations are particular to our tradition and may differ from other forms of traditional and dogmatic rabbinical lore.

Liber יסוד, meaning *foundation* in Hebrew, provides the initiate with the major concepts and tools so that he can understand the principles within the Kabbalistic tradition and deepen his studies through the teachings of the Aset Ka and other published Hebrew literature. It is a start, not an end.

Prior to this study, it is also important to understand that, in the Kabbalah, the concept of divinity found when referring to a *creator* does not designate the religious God found in monotheistic theology, but a higher level of experience that each of us can attain through wisdom - a true form of spiritual enlightenment.

This is especially true in the case of יהוה or *YHWH* - the Tetragrammaton. Wrongly transliterated as *Jehovah* in many texts, this definition does not refer to an anthropomorphic deity like the one found in Christianity and modern Judaism. It is an abstract concept to embody the indefinable nature of divinity, expressed in here by the four letters of Yod י, He ה, Vav ו and He ה. These simple letters hold such important significance and meaning that, when together, they are rarely pronounced by the traditional Hebrew scholars or written in Jewish religious literature due to the sacredness attributed to this formula in their tradition. Instead, the word יהוה - Yod He Vav He - is commonly seen being transliterated and uttered by the use of different words like *Lord* among other references to a divine force.

"Seek him that maketh the seven stars and Orion, and turneth the shadow of death into the morning, and maketh the day dark with night: that calleth for the waters of the sea, and poureth them out upon the face of the earth: The Lord is his name."

Amos 5:8[1]

This passage from the Book of Amos, part of the Tanakh - the Hebrew Bible - and the Old Testament of the Christian Bible is a fine example on the literary adulteration of the Tetragrammaton. Some earlier translations have used Jehovah instead of *Lord*, both working as transliterations of יהוה that the Jews don't pronounce due to its sacredness in their tradition. Under the light of understanding this passage holds an even deeper meaning, as by replacing the word *Lord* with the correct Hebrew letters we have the unveiling of the secret on how the ancients were aware that the Tetragrammaton of the Kabbalah has an intimate connection with the mysteries of Orion. Furthermore, it conceals a hidden allusion to the four alchemical elements, where the *shadow of death* refers to Fire, what *maketh the day dark with night* is Air, the *waters of the sea* represent Water and the *face of the earth* naturally relates with Earth.

The Tetragrammaton, which is embodied in literature and magick by the four letters of the Hebrew alphabet, expresses the four layers of the manifest Universe as well as the four elementals that comprise the foundations of reality and spiritual alchemy - Fire, Water, Air and Earth. It also reflects the *Planes of Existence* found in Asetianism[2], and appropriate analogies will be better understood in the following text when learning about the *Tree of Life* as a spiritual diagram of both inner and outer realities.

In the study of the nature of divinity it remains a point of extreme importance to understand and accept this abstract definition of deity, particularly when exploring the Kabbalah, and not to confuse it with the modern view of godhood. Among the many descriptions like Jehovah, God, Adonai and Lord, a more suitable and meaningful word used in ancient religious scriptures when referring to divinity is *Elohim*. This ancient word shrouded in mystery holds the missing connection to the multidimensional view of deity as found in the Kabbalah, as the Hebrew word is a feminine noun followed by a masculine termination, while being both grammatically singular and plural.[3] This philological detail hides an important secret behind the word *Elohim*, as it refers not to a single omnipotent God like the one found in the limited dogma of monotheistic religions, but actually embodies in a singular word the manifestation of many Gods expressed through feminine and masculine principles, which are so accurately represented in the pantheon of Ancient Egypt. An interesting hint concerning this powerful word is found in the *Book of Exodus*, the second book present in both the Hebrew and Christian Bible, where *Elohim* is used to describe nothing less than the Gods of Egypt.

To properly study the wisdom of the Kabbalah in a serious and mature form one must realize that we are dealing with highly abstract concepts that are used as subtle representations of a reality that is in fact impossible to be accurately expressed by the means of words and symbols and, to some extent, unable to be fully comprehended with a regular mindset. I ask that during this process of learning and adaptation to a reality of symbolism and spiritual abstraction that the student keep an open mind and raise his level of awareness to another dimension - that of the Spirit.

Marques' Spiritual Kaleidoscope

Anyone familiar on an elementary level with the Asetian tradition and its Ancient Egyptian legacy may at first wonder why broadening his spiritual culture through the wisdom of the Kabbalah holds any significance. First of all, any apprentice of the Asetian path worthy of such a name would by now have come to the realization that the Asetian framework develops around the concept of Understanding through the means of Wisdom. This increased awareness manifests through a process of exploration, committed learning and practice. The initiate of Asetianism is renown for the depth of his knowledge and this does not apply to a single subject or branch of science. Asetianists are constantly encouraged to learn about every form of knowledge and culture in order to develop a greater understanding of the higher Truth as unveiled behind the big picture. Different views will provide answers to different questions, as each culture has a small limited piece of the spiritual cosmos developed from its very own background and experience. Each tradition on its own, while isolated from other knowledge and the chaos of opposed views, is limited and hence incomplete. The importance of such exploration to personal evolution and in the process of finding Self will become increasingly more evident as the student progresses through different forms of initiation and matures spiritually.

> *"If we intend to take our occult studies seriously and make of them anything more than desultory light reading, we must choose our system and carry it out faithfully until we arrive, if not at its ultimate goal, at any rate at definite practical results and a permanent enhancement of consciousness. After this has been achieved we may, not without advantage, experiment*

✝

with the methods that have been developed upon other Paths, and build up an eclectic technique and philosophy therefrom; but the student who sets out to be an eclectic before he has made himself an expert will never be anything more than a dabbler."

Dion Fortune

This brief passage from occultist Dion Fortune on her text on the Kabbalah is quite representative of a problem that many modern occultists encounter during their first years of practice. People often skim the surface of various spiritual traditions to incorporate different elements into their own eclectic practices that better suits their needs and expectations. Through a brief study of several books related with an esoteric road people already assume that they understand the path and know enough to make fair judgment on what it has to offer, as well as to borrow and adapt its traditional ideas into their own personal view and practice without ever mastering such knowledge. This results in recognition of the basic symbology found at the surface of many traditions but a complete lack of understanding on the essence and wisdom present in those paths. Every honest occult tradition of the world takes years to study and dedicated practice to master; it cannot be understood at a workshop or mastered through a book, as it must be lived and experienced first hand.

While I always recommend the study of every form of knowledge and occult traditions, it becomes relevant to explain that such method of self-development requires a deeper understanding of the mysteries and paths being explored and that, while a profound knowledge of different cultures and traditions is highly beneficial to the student of the occult, simple examinations of a path may only provide further confusion and will not gift the seeker with the required understanding so that he can use said path in his personal practice.

In a society where people make frivolous use of occult symbolism that they do not comprehend and profess to follow paths and study traditions they never practiced or understood, an occultist must strive to be a good and sincere representation of whatever road of wisdom he follows and studies, as often the loudest people found in different paths and modern communities are a terrible representation of the essence and values of the path they believe to follow and should never be used as an element to understand a specific tradition. Spirituality is independent of opinion and social identity, as it exists on its own. Individual character, viewpoint and interpretation can never define a tradition.

> *"If we are silent, we can listen, and so learn; but if we*
> *are talking, the gates of entrance to the mind are closed."*
>
> Dion Fortune

A concept frequently found in Asetianism and often misunderstood by the non-initiated is that of *Silence*. The ability to accept and master quietness, stillness and mental plenitude is a vital tool for the serious adept of the magickal arts and an essential step in any profound spiritual quest. This *silence* is not expressed through a limited existence of isolation or the ecclesiastical silence found in monastic life, but manifests the inner power to shield from mundane noise, deceptive echoes and distracting influences in order to be able to listen to the pure voice found within that speaks through subtlety. Without attaining such level of growth through the power of silence, communion with Self is not possible. This idea is well carved in the thought of every gnostic spiritual tradition, holding the long-established occult principle which postulates that someone loud can never be considered a true adversary or ally, as inner weakness is exposed though the inability to learn, for only those that can listen in silence can be trusted as real students.

I hope that my approach to manifold expressions of wisdom and different layers of the occult will motivate the reader to explore other forms of knowledge and not just the teachings that are directly tied to the Asetian nature or any other path of their preference and to do so without fear or dogma, with a mindset and commitment to an honest further development. It is of central importance while studying other paths to do so with a genuine thirst for knowledge and passion for learning, placing the focus within and not driven by outside influence or the perspective of ego, as when the inspiration is drawn from the indulgence of vanity or the fear within the subconscious, true learning is not possible. Occult wisdom is one of the most deceiving forms of gnosis, as it will only teach the truthful while guiding the fools into a shimmering road of presumptuous glitter.

Other traditions and metaphysical systems will unveil alternative interpretations of the Universe and reality, providing what I have called a *Spiritual Kaleidoscope*; a multilayered and multidimensional understanding of Life, spirituality and human thought. This advanced level of understanding and awareness achieved through a holistic and nonjudgmental study of the many layers of spirituality - the *Kaleidoscope* - represents a powerful inner technology to be used in the never-ending quest for wisdom and enlightenment, a technique that I have continuously taught and inspired within the students of the Aset Ka. Ultimately, if the foundation is strong, the study and understanding of different religions and occult traditions will not shake the initiate in his passion and commitment to the Asetian path, but will actually provide him with renewed resolve, sentiment and understanding towards the

✝

teachings of Aset, as he realizes through first hand experience how countless other traditions and cultures simply have pieces of the hidden puzzle that is Asetianism. This is not to say that every practice or belief can be absorbed into our own practices or seen under our light. Some knowledge is genuinely incompatible and misleading, or worse yet, simply downright fake.

Having contact with false knowledge, just like dealing with dishonest people, is also an important lesson in the path of growth and a learning tool that should not be underestimated. Learning to recognize what is real from what is not, as what is true from what is false, represents a level of awareness that the student of the occult must learn to master for the sake of his own evolution. We enforce and advise the study of all forms of knowledge, thought and practice, as we strongly believe that experience only allows for the initiate to realize how beautiful and precious the Asetian culture truly is. That alone is an initiation in itself.

Hebrew Language

Hebrew is the language of the Kabbalah. Developed in the Middle East as a Semitic language it is known to be one of the oldest languages in the world. Currently one of the two official languages of Israel, along with Arabic, Hebrew is well known among the adepts of the occult and subject of serious study in many secret societies due to its mystical alphabet formed by twenty-two letters or sigils. The Jews call it Leshon Hakodesh - לשון הקודש - meaning the *Sacred Language.*

The number *twenty-two* of the letters found in the Hebrew alphabet is not arbitrary. It manifests as an echo of the twenty-two paths connecting the different spiritual emanations - sephiroth - in the

Tree of Life, as well as the twenty-two *Major Arcana* found in the traditional Tarot, but more on that later.

To understand the formation of the Hebrew alphabet under a Kabbalistic perspective we shall imagine the singular embodiment of divine manifestation, before the Universe was formed, as being represented by a single point.[4] That singular point, a coherent dot in the void of chaos, represents the hidden potential to manifest the whole Universe. It constitutes the intact complete existence: no reality, no dimensions, no nature - just a point, the unformed divinity.

If this point in the cradle of the Gods would suddenly gain consciousness and awareness, at the verge of the creation of the Universe, it would stretch its energies left and right to the further reaches of the now forming Universe. This philosophical alchemy would create the first dimension - length. Following this primordial awakening the point would expand its awareness up and down, to the highest and the lowest realms of infinity. Height, the second dimension, would have been brought into existence. At last, the essence of the point would reach from front to back, creating the third and last dimension of our tridimensional reality - depth. In this philosophical approach the Kabbalah describes the Universe as being manifested out of three elemental realities, describing not only the root frameworks of the cosmos but also the foundations of sacred geometry. The number *three* then becomes the first number of primordial manifestation.

At this point a tridimensional reality was formed and, for empirical examination, through mathematical science and the principles of geometry, we can define it as a cube. The structure that embodies the Universe was given form out of the three basic dimensions - length, height and depth. If we pay closer attention to this newborn reality - the mystical cube - we realize that it exists by the means of seven frameworks; the six faces of the cube and the primordial dot in its center as the divine expression that manifested the whole Universe. Through this paradigm we reach at the number *seven* as the second number of primordial manifestation.

Studying this conceptual cube in further detail we realize that those seven universal frameworks must be supported by something, or some force, otherwise they would simply disperse into chaos. There must be some power holding them together, giving them meaning, through a coherent and balanced existence. That materializes through the line segments expressed as the edges of the cube. Those thin vibrational lines hold the faces of our cube in place, keeping order in the Universe. Such invisible filaments express the third and last number of primordial manifestation: the number *twelve*. In the Asetian tradition we call it Maat, the Ancient Egyptian personification of balance and order.

Finally, we can define the Universe through the unification of the three primordial dimensions, the seven frameworks of existence as the six faces of the cube plus the initial point and the twelve faces of Maat as the edges of the cube. This is an infinitely expanding reality with no real boundaries or form except those of perception. As a manifest Universe that is the natural expression of reality, like in all forms of creation, the cube is not limited by human geometry.

$$3 + 7 + 12 = 22$$

That is the Kabbalistic formula for the creation of the Universe and the alchemical secret behind the twenty-two letters of the Hebrew alphabet. This realm of esoteric numerology also

✝

expresses several mysteries behind the wisdom of the Tarot, the initiatory keys of the Universe, the foundations of Biology and the rules of science.

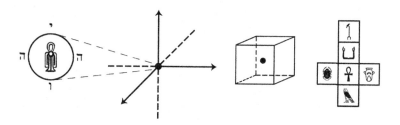

At this point the Asetianists studying this *Liber* with due focus and attention may be starting to see some order and meaning in the apparent chaos of the Kabbalah, as the number *three* found in this mystical alchemy can be seen as a philosophical expression of the *Three Primordials* and the number *seven* represents the *Seven Sacred Pillars* of the Asetian tradition. Like I previously stated, nothing is arbitrary.

The three Lineages - three dimensions of the soul - give form to the act of creation and through them manifest the seven frameworks that command the Universe - Ankh, Khepri, Ka, Was, Ba and Ib as the six faces of the sacred cube plus Tiet as the divine dot at the core of existence; the blood of Aset.

Delving deeper into the mysteries of the Hebrew alphabet we realize that by separating the letters into those three distinctive groups[5], according to the formation of the Universe, we find the three alchemical elements of initiation, the seven planets of the ancients and the twelve constellations of the zodiac.

The three primary or mother letters, also known as the elemental letters, are Aleph א, Mem מ and Shin ש - representing Air,

Water and Fire. Some may wonder why Earth is not represented but it happens that, in Kabbalistic mysticism and spiritual alchemy, Earth is seen as a lesser element of inferior purity. During the study of *Liber Sigillum 333*, particularly in the chapter on the *Sarcophagus of Flesh*, the reader shall understand the occult implications of such reasoning and the fundament for its neglecting aspect in the formation of the world.

The seven secondary or double letters are Beth ב, Gimel ג, Daleth ד, Kaph כ, Pe פ, Resh ר and Tav ת. They represent the planets of the ancients, which are also known as the seven classical planets of antiquity - Mercury, Moon, Venus, Jupiter, Mars, the Sun and Saturn.

For the learned occultist, the connection with each letter and their precise positioning on the Tree of Life and the Major Arcana of the Tarot has profound astrological implications in the interpretation of different esoteric systems. It is relevant to explain that the Sun is not a planet at all in astronomical nomenclature but a star, nor is the Moon seen as a true planet by contemporary astronomy; however, both were studied as planets by the ancient alchemists, and although they were astronomically incorrect those aspects represented important symbolical and conceptual references in their geocentric view.

In the Asetian tradition these seven frameworks are properly identified as the *Sacred Pillars*, important keys of mystery to understand Life and its manifestation in the Universe.

The twelve tertiary or simple letters are He ה, Vav ו, Zain ז, Cheth ח, Teth ט, Yod י, Lamed ל, Nun נ, Samekh ס, Ayin ע, Tsadi צ and Qoph ק. They represent the constellations of the zodiac - Aries, Taurus, Gemini, Cancer, Leo, Virgo, Libra, Scorpio, Sagittarius, Capricorn, Aquarius and Pisces.

	Name	Hebrew	Arabic	Magick
1	Aleph	א	ا	Air
2	Mem	מ	م	Water
3	Shin	ש	ش	Fire
4	Beth	ב	ب	Mercury
5	Gimel	ג	ج	Moon
6	Daleth	ד	د	Venus
7	Kaph	כ	ك	Jupiter
8	Pe	פ	ف	Mars
9	Resh	ר	ر	Sun
10	Tav	ת	ت	Saturn
11	He	ה	ه	Aries
12	Vav	ו	و	Taurus
13	Zain	ז	ز	Gemini
14	Cheth	ח	ح	Cancer
15	Teth	ט	ط	Leo
16	Yod	י	ي	Virgo
17	Lamed	ל	ل	Libra
18	Nun	נ	ن	Scorpio
19	Samekh	ס	س	Sagittarius
20	Ayin	ע	ع	Capricorn
21	Tsadi	צ	ص	Aquarius
22	Qoph	ק	ق	Pisces

✝

Tree of Life

The Tree of Life is the central device in Kabbalistic technology. Known as *Eitz Chaim* in Hebrew - עץ חיים -, it is surrounded with meaning and rooted in symbolism. The proper interpretation and study of this magickal device has eluded occultists for centuries, being part of the teachings found throughout countless mystery schools of our past, present and certainly the future.

Published for the first time in 1652 in the work of Jesuit scholar Athanasius Kircher, entitled *Oedipus Ægyptiacus*, the image of the Tree is not just a symbol or a collection of sigils. Instead, it is a diagram of the manifest Universe: a model of creation and evolution. It represents Life but it also mirrors Death and the perpetual continuum. The interpretation and study of the Tree of Life should not be strict or shrouded in the limited light of rules but as dynamic and mutable as the realm of thought, since it cannot be properly understood if attached to dogma and the restricted boundaries of concept. The student is therefore advised not to focus solely on its connection with the Asetian Lineages and spiritual expression through the Holy Trinity - Serpent, Scarab and Scorpion -, while at the same time keeping such understanding in the scope of awareness. As meditative gnosis the glyph presents the hierarchical unfolding of consciousness, structured in order to break the advanced psychology of sentient beings into smaller layers possible of coherent study and to be analyzed by the focused mind.

The function and application of the wisdom deduced from the Tree is diverse and its occult scope should always be approached as a tool and multilayered chart that can be adapted and interpreted under different frameworks and to express different manifestations. Its reflex of the triple Asetian nature, although a potent spiritual tool, it is just one of the many applications of this symbol to be found in occult wisdom. While studying the Kabbalah it is important to remain aware that tools and interpretations such as the Tree of Life may be approached as another reflection of the Asetian nature through its many universal faces, but it would be incorrect to approach Asetianism and the study of its tradition as an expression of the knowledge manifested by the Tree. The Kabbalah and its symbolical structure of Life and layers of existence can be studied as complex esoteric expressions of the universal Asetian path and through that study to grasp further depth in Hebrew mysticism and its cultural legacy, but Asetianism should not be understood as a reflection of the Tree. In fact, on a first approach to the study of the Kabbalah some occultists may benefit from not overly focusing on the placement of the Lineage archetypes in the Tree as the lacking of certain mystery keys may raise confusion and lead to wrong interpretations. The Kabbalistic system can be studied without delving into its Asetian connections and influence, in an independent exploration that still retains its occult validity and power to be used in magickal practice.

The human mind has a tendency to categorize all information as a way to better understand and organize thought, and that makes people raise walls around different concepts instead of trying a more synergistic approach to occult wisdom. This leads to great misunderstanding when it comes to spirituality, as we are dealing with a realm of thought that cannot be defined or limited by the rules of definition and concept. To impose limitations in mystical thought and to restrict the understanding of transcendence by a need for categorization is limiting wisdom in its very essence. Although we make use of definition and concept in order to be able to pass certain layers of knowledge to other initiates it becomes important to realize that those very same definitions are limited and restricted, being ultimately impossible for them to carry the full weight of the gnosis

✝

they intend to convey. This is particularly relevant while studying such intricate traditions as Asetianism and the Kabbalah, as their spiritual and philosophical elements exist in the realm of transcendence where the only path to develop a proper - although still limited - level of understanding is through a holistic approach that interconnects all elements and reveals the world as a complex, unlimited and indefinable reality. Magickal sigils represent a fine example on the devices that require this approach in order to be properly used in esoteric practice, which becomes particularly clear while studying the Tree of Life. In this case, the esoteric glyph is much more than just a symbol and it should be understood as an actual spiritual technology to be explored in practice, study and meditation; one that if limitations and barriers are imposed quickly loses much of its hidden power.

Sometimes students don't immediately understand the meaning of the word *technology* when used in connection with spirituality, the occult and the magickal arts. Technology in any form represents a branch of knowledge that interconnects specific technical terminology and concepts in their relationship with life and the surrounding environment, which are often associated with science and engineering but are also strongly present in the scholarly fields of the occult and art. Although vastly unknown within popular occult circles, spiritual and esoteric technologies are an important part of traditional occult studies and have been created, developed and improved inside different Orders since the earlier days in Ancient Egypt to the initiatory societies still present in modern time. Spiritual technologies make use of esoteric devices that can be explored and applied by initiates of the mysteries in order to aid in the understanding of Life, the Universe and the secrets of inner Self. The Kabbalah and its Tree of Life represent one of those powerful technologies, but there are many others like the usage of sigils and Asetian talismans to the study of metaphysics, energy work and subtle anatomy; all different technologies available to the occultist that comprise his arsenal of wisdom and the tools to craft the foundations of the world.

Only in gradual steady progression the wisdom found in the Tree can be unfolded and properly assimilated. Connections that might not make sense in the initial study will eventually open the gates of possibility after further exploration. Passion for the Kabbalah represents a commitment of years in its study, a reason why so many fail to understand it. Although so powerful and illuminating when mastered, this kind of knowledge will not please those seeking brief answers and easy paths. As mentioned in the introduction to this book, anyone with such a mindset shall only find frustration and confusion while studying this work or exploring the Kabbalah through any other serious publication. To those not concerned about time and immediate satisfaction, the ones willing to pour their energies into the colossal undertaking of esoteric learning, they are bound to find through this gnosis an empowering tool to understand the Universe and themselves, as the keys in the Tree can be used to explore macrocosmically and microcosmically. If the reader does not nurture that same passion, strength and dedication to the noble mysteries of the occult arts, it might be wiser to close these pages, store the book in a safe location and return to it if renewed determination is found a few years later.

The Tree of Life, as a composite symbol, can be used as an instrument of cosmic understanding and, in that sense, it is a highly scientific glyph. The occultist must learn to use the Tree as a device of analysis and research, like a medical doctor makes use of the stethoscope to locate signs of illness, the biologist goes to a microscope to understand nature, or an astronomer observes the cosmos through a modern telescope. The secrets of the Tarot, as an initiatory expression of the wisdom hidden in the Tree of Life, manifest such a potent spiritual tool by the means of art and symbols. When used together, they become a lens to see the Universe, a compass to chart the path and a language to enhance spiritual understanding. They are formulae to calculate reality.

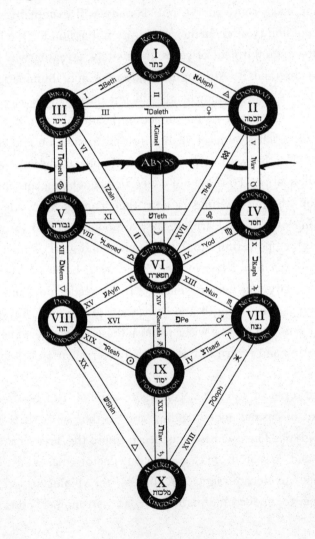

The Tree of Life is formed by ten sephiroth connected through twenty-two initiatory paths. Each sephirah - the singular for sephiroth - is a stage of spiritual enlightenment and magickal mindset, therefore only reached by a specific road of initiation. Each initiatory path that holds the key to open the doors to a sephirah is very important. This occult process of self-development is very powerful and develops through meditation and ritual as the initiate spiritually walks the paths of the Tree, defeats the terrible guardians at the doors of each sephirah and crosses its gates into the inner temple. The fact that there are exactly twenty-two paths in the Tree is far from random, and now you may start to see its relationship with the twenty-two letters of the Hebrew alphabet and how all this wisdom connects with the formation of the physical Universe by the manifestation of matter. This alchemical process of reaching the stage of matter - the physical realm - from an entirely spiritual reality made of energy is what we describe in Asetianism as the mystery *From Purity to Dust*, and you will learn more about it in the following pages. The twenty-two paths in the Tree of Life represent each of the twenty-two *Major Arcana* of the Tarot, therefore expressing profound initiatory keys to the understanding of the whole Tree, making Kabbalistic numerology and gematria an extensive subject of occult science.

Proper study, interpretation and understanding of the Tree are not possible without contemplation. The knowledge of the symbolism and spiritual terminology provided in this *Liber* is essential, but its usage is limited if not completed with the work of meditation. As you might have noticed by now, the spiritual significance of the Tree is dual, as it represents the formation of the Universe from energy to matter, and mirrors the initiatory nature of the soul. It describes the nature of the macrocosm while at the same time mirrors the microcosm of your inner Self. These two interpretations are essential

✝

to understand the wisdom of the Kabbalah and they complement each other, holding the key to understand your own place in the Universe at a specific moment in time.

Look within to see the Tree.
Look at the Tree to see yourself.

The structure of the Tree of Life is organized in such a way that the occultist can use it to study the locked doors of the soul, to master thought and Will, to unveil the path of initiation and to understand reality. Through its symbolism it can be perceived as mirroring the triple nature of the Asetian path, the decomposing of subtle energy into its microcosmic elements, the structure of the chakra of the Hindus and the Shen centers of the Asetians, as well as the steps of wisdom and enlightenment found in the Western philosophical schools.

The purpose of the Kabbalah and this introductory *Liber* is to provide the student with the mental and spiritual tools to constantly evolve into a higher state of consciousness and through this process to reach a higher level of wisdom and understanding. In Asetianism the initiate works towards the removal of ego, self-deceit and psychological conditioning created by society and cultural background, so that by the end of the spiritual process there is only raw Self left to acknowledge. When this initiatory state of awareness is attained, the true nature and individuality of Self is finally revealed and understanding of inner truth is unveiled. Only then is real communion with the divine possible. At this point of spiritual maturity prejudice from society holds no power and the mundane opinion of ignorance becomes a confirmation on the accomplishments of the initiate and a tool for further teaching. It is a powerful form of

✝

awakening at the root of a groundbreaking sensation of freedom often described by Asetianists committed to path of the Wise. This supreme state of liberation cannot be explained by words or defined by art, but only felt by those who have experienced it.

From Purity to Dust

Studying the formation of the Tree of Life is a complicated but essential mental process to understand Kabbalistic philosophy. Its interpretation and the relationship between each element of the Tree is highly complex and takes years of study to understand, so no detail should be underestimated as such teachings need the action of time in order to properly mature in the mind.

I will reduce each major element of the glyph to its basic foundation and explain the metaphysical development of the final Tree through a simple process of energy transmutation, from the highest vibrational stage into the lowest form of manifestation - the physical realm. This will make clear to the initiate how the process of mystical creation unfolds, as well as how the perpetual cycle of energy manifests through its degrading process of higher vibration in ethereal form into consecutive lower vibrational states until it finally descends into matter where it becomes perceivable by the common mind.

Through the study and understanding of the full process, the occultist opens the inner door to consciously manipulate and interfere with each stage of subtle and mental manifestation, exposing the art of energy work as practiced at an advanced level of magick.

Beyond the realm of matter, thought and even energy, lies the concept of divinity and what can be described as the purest form of existence: Indefinable. Incomprehensible. Infinite. Timeless.

✝

This indecipherable embodiment of divinity is what is known in the Kabbalah as *Ain Soph,* אין סוף in Hebrew, sometimes also spelled *Ein Sof.* It is a conceptual representation of something immeasurable and beyond understanding to the mind while bonded to the physical reality of incarnation and life sustained in a material body. Ain Soph, the undefinable expression of deity that is at the same time nothingness and everything, is sometimes represented in the Kabbalah by three so-called *veils of negativity,* known as *Ain, Ain Soph* and *Ain Soph Aur.* At this stage, for simplicity of understanding, and as these three layers of unspoken divinity are in fact one and the supreme expression of oneness, we will refer to them simply as Ain Soph.

Below the not always represented invisible veils of Ain Soph reside the ten spheres of initiation known as *sephiroth -* סְפִירוֹת in Hebrew. For the occultist to explore the magick and power of each sephirah, contemplation and meditation are essential but not enough to achieve an enlightened understanding of its nature. It is also required to plunge the psyche deeply into the realm of the sephirah under exploration and experience its energy and lessons first-hand by the means of ritual, metaphysics and transcendence. Only after touching a sephirah with your magickal hands may you understand its secret language.

The first three sephiroth are very special and must be approached differently from the rest of the emanations present in the Tree. They are known as Kether, Chokmah and Binah and represent the only sephiroth located above the Abyss, expressing the archetypical emanations that will unfold the rest of the full Tree.

In Kabbalistic philosophy the spiritual process of their formation is understood under a mechanism of energy transmutation akin to what is experienced in metaphysical practice. This process, although subjective in its approach, is important to understand and we will now study it in detail in order to comprehend how does the full Tree of Life manifest into reality.

Starting with Kether, meaning Crown in Hebrew, at the very top of the Tree we have the first conscious emanation from the divine - Ain Soph - into our perceivable Universe; the actual personification of unspoken divinity, now definable and objective. In the fabric of the soul Kether appears as the quintessence of absolute oneness, the most transcendent layer of Self. As Kether is manifested through primordial creation, its first spiritual realization is conscious awareness of its own existence; the singular absolute truth - it exists. As we are dwelling in an ethereal realm of philosophy and energy, the very thought of acknowledging and accepting Self creates another sephirah in its image; a reflection of its self-awareness known as Chokmah, meaning Wisdom in Hebrew - in this case, Wisdom of Self and its absolute reality. However, scientific principles as the law of conservation of energy found in modern physics postulate that energy cannot be created but only transformed, and the same is true with the principles of metaphysics that were studied by the ancients. So these emanations of pure energy are not transmutable through an act of mirroring, but instead manifested in a process of fragmentation. This observation leads to the philosophical realization that Chokmah is not in fact an accurate mirror of Kether, but its own distorted view of itself. Awareness of this primordial truth, where the image of Self is not the same as true Self, is then manifested as Binah - the silent bringer of truth -, meaning Understanding in Hebrew.

Wisdom alone is incomplete if not mastered through Understanding, and only then, when united, they can Crown the supreme truth. The three sephiroth complete each other and form the highest representation of divinity: the indefinable Ain Soph. One *mirrors* into two and *becomes* three - the first Kabbalistic and Kemetic formula of creation: an accurate representation of the divine trinity and the triple nature of Life.

As confusing as this may sound, the reader should remain aware that this represents an abstract visualization of the process as interpreted by Kabbalistic mystics and should be interpreted as a philosophical theory and not a literal account of the Tree's formation.

Also worthy of reference is that while the first three sephiroth are also one single emanation when united, they all reside in an ethereal realm where there is no definition of time and space, so although we describe their formation through the process of energy transmutation explained above, they actually manifest in the exact same moment, and it would not be conceptually accurate to think of one as prior or older than another. Under an Asetian perspective it becomes clear how the concept of Kether resonates with the philosophical representation of Horus, where even its original Hebrew translation to *Crown* seems to hint at a past connection with Ancient Egyptian mythology where Horus was the personification of the Pharaoh and sometimes described in religious literature simply as *The Crown*.

The first three sephiroth, often described as the supernal triad, exemplify the triple nature of reality that the Asetians have taught for centuries; the threefold path through which energy can manifest and how spiritual life comes into existence if it could be studied under a metaphysical microscope. They are an accurate personification of Unity in its most absolute form: the magickal formula where a *pure one equals three*. These three sephiroth are silently echoed in nature by the three stars in the belt of Orion, watching life unfold through its thrones in the sky; spiritual reflections of the three Primordials as the perfect echo from the essence of each Lineage in the spiritual bloodline of the Gods, glimmering in the dark cloak of the night.

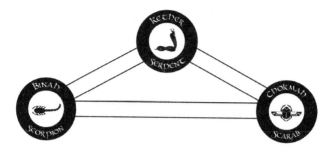

The three primal emanations of divinity appear in an area of the Tree meant to represent a different reality from the rest of the glyph, an ethereal world located above the veil of mystery that the Kabbalists designated as the Abyss or Da'ath. This mystical cloak of both light and darkness separates the realm of divinity and the land of the dead - the Duat from the Ancient Egyptian mysteries - from the lower realities of the astral plane and the world of matter; both permanently existing below the Abyss.

If we approach the supernal triad as one single unit, we can apply the same process of development that we have observed in its very own formation from the veils of negativity. The attaining of consciousness by the three higher emanations creates an imperfect reflection of their nature and energy in the realm below the Abyss, hence forming the sephiroth Chesed by reflection of Chokmah, Geburah by reflection of Binah and, finally, Tiphareth by reflection of Kether.

These newborn emanations are the sephiroth four, five and six, which translate from Hebrew to Mercy, Strength and Beauty, and they embody the higher manifestation of the sephiroth one, two and three in the *real* Universe, below the mystical veil of Da'ath, representing the hexagram of creation and mirroring the timeless principle of Thoth *"As Above, so Below."*

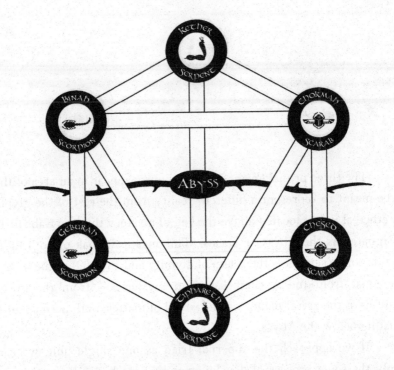

As the active thoughts of the reader might have conspired by now, the lower manifestations of the higher trinity cannot really be an accurate representation of the first three divine sephiroth. Even if we managed to ignore the metaphysical laws of energy transmutation, it would still be foolish to presume that pure divine archetypes could be made manifest in the known Universe, retaining the same conceptual purity. Reality itself exercises influence on their light, changing their properties and energy as it does with every single one of us.

Awareness of this fact, just like in the original process, instantly manifests a third trinity below the previous one, with the sephiroth seven, eight and nine, completing the set of initiatory seats above the physical world; six below the Abyss, already part of this Universe, and three above Da'ath, in the indefinable realm of infinity. The newly formed spiritual spheres are Netzach meaning Victory by reflection of

✝

Chesed, Hod meaning Splendor by reflection of Geburah and Yesod meaning Foundation by reflection of Tiphareth.

The sephirah nine, Yesod, is the lowest manifestation of the one, Kether, before reaching the plane of matter and losing its subtle essence, being connected with the concept and name of this esoteric document, called *Liber* יסוד, meaning *Liber Yesod* or *Liber Foundation*. This sephirah holds central significance in occult studies as it represents one of the first initiatory steps and subtle thrones to conquer in advanced magickal practice.

Yesod is the psychic center and the primary filter through which the occultist experiences the metaphysical phenomena and extrasensory perception; it represents the first gate to energy work and the actual temple in which energy manipulation is consciously achieved. The sephirah Yesod as the cosmic engine behind the machinery of the Universe potentiates the sensitivity over the subtle, located a layer above the locks of matter found in Malkuth, in the same way that Hod embodies the throne of ritual magick and the gate to power through mystical knowledge.

The last sephirah, number ten, is called Malkuth, which means Kingdom in Hebrew, and it represents the physical world - the material plane. This is the final step of decadence and where the soul ultimately reaches after liberating most of its energy and spiritual properties in the paths above through the process of incarnation and physical birth. It is the fragmentation of energy from its highest and purest form into the lowest embodiment; the incarnation of matter.

These concepts along with the unveiling of their spiritual mystery will be further developed in the study of *Liber Sigillum 333*, when addressing the *Sarcophagus of Flesh*.

✝

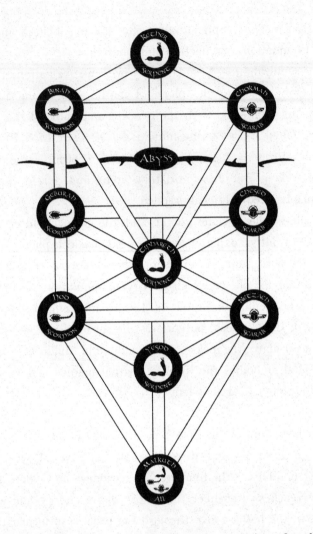

In Malkuth, the distinguishable characteristics of each Asetian Lineage blend with each other, being many times lost in confusion and hard to properly validate. Asetians in the spiritual stage of Malkuth are the unawakened, many times lost in the mundane life and unaware of their inner truth and hidden flame, but yet still retaining their divine spark in potential.

This sphere also represents the uninitiated adept - an Asetianist or the follower of another spiritual path - when the journey of enlightenment starts. It is a realm of unawareness, doubt and confusion, where energy and the subtle realms are hidden. It is the land of the living: the only place where the physical body actually exists.

In this context the Tree of Life represents the core of each initiate, as in terms of spiritual archetype the Serpent, Scarab and Scorpion all live inside each individual Asetian. This is one of the inner mysteries often misunderstood by the students of Asetian spirituality.

It is of paramount understanding that each and every Asetian has an imprint from Horus within the soul and his Divine Self represented in the Crown of Kether. However, this essence expressed through the first sephirah is not something perceivable or definable from a regular level of consciousness, as it is located much above the so-called Higher Self that still resides below the Abyss.

The Higher Self is the highest expression of each individual while still incarnated in the realm of flesh, but not the ultimate reality as that is embodied through his Divine Self above the gates of Da'ath, being part of the indefinable mystery of the Duat; the land of divinity and the highest vibrational plane before the plunge into nothingness, a place without positive or negative, past or future, but where all shapes and forms unify as One.

So the triple formula of Orion found in this system replicates the shift of mindset and energy throughout life and initiation, from the highest and purest form of three emanations above the veil of consciousness to their mundane and incarnated counterparts that degrade over the Tree of Life, reaching the lowest and unaware realm of Malkuth; the Kingdom. Once in Malkuth there is no longer a true spiritual identity, as the Self is so asleep and polluted, centered in the microcosm of the material world, which no longer holds the vision and awareness to realize that there is a whole rich spiritual realm above - represented in the full Tree of Life - and that all of it is in fact an essential part of himself.

The study of such gnosis aids the seeker in how to walk through the twenty-two initiatory roads in order to achieve communion with each sephirah in a state of spiritual enlightenment. Across the long journey of each personal path the student naturally shifts his awareness and mindset through different focus within the Tree, sometimes ending up relocated to a specific sephirah of thought without conscious effort or training, as they all represent universal spiritual thrones. In terms of personal growth and spiritual evolution, walking through the paths of initiation and reaching a specific sephirah does not mean that you are stalled or accomplished in that sphere. The state of each sephirah above Malkuth is not permanent, as everything in spiritual life is in constant motion and change, moved by chaos, nature and magick. So the sephiroth do not represent planes to master, but schools to learn from. They are not expressed through permanent states of enlightenment, but rather impermanent states of awareness and focus, achieved by successfully walking the twenty-two initiatory paths within the Tree of Life, being accepted by the ethereal guardians of each sephirah and to be trusted within its temple - becoming initiated in its mysteries. The temple of each sephirah embodies different attunements of perception in magickal seats of power, connected by the initiatory archetypes of creation.

As we reach at the fully developed scheme of the Tree of Life in this study I will now ask the reader to focus his attention on the triple vertical alignment of the sephiroth. That ordered arrangement defines three clear pillars parallel to each other, related to each Lineage and

✝

manifested by three sephiroth each - Malkuth is not really integrated in any of the spiritual pillars as it is located in a lower realm, that of physical matter.

They express what is studied within initiatory societies as *The Pillars of the Mysteries*; the left side of the Tree embodies feminine energies and the right side emanates the male principles, while the center unifies both male and female - described in the occult as the secret path of *The Middle Pillar*. On the Left there is darkness, mystery, introspection and the secrets of the unconscious, while on the Right there is light, openness, clarity and the virtues of the conscious mind. They govern the occult foundations of the Left Hand Path and the Right Hand Path, as two opposed beams leading to the same cave hidden in the ether: darkness and light, two faces of the same force - Equilibrium.

The ancient sages have also described the pillars in terms of polarity - the left being negative and the right being positive by tradition - and although such definition is valid in terms of metaphysics and magickal practice I have avoided delving deeper into the specific details of positive and negative energy frameworks, due to its potential for misunderstanding in earlier studies by the initiates with an inadequate cultural and philosophical background that may be conditioned to improper interpretation on the subjects of negative polarity and magickal destruction in spiritual alchemy. The pillars in each side of the Tree express a concept described in Asetianism as the *universal duality.*

Every manifestation is dual and the forces of nature, being always two-sided, unfold in an universal progression of two that as you can see, under the spiritual microscope, are actually an emanation of three; the Left, the Right and the Middle, that unifies both - oneness and completion.

Observing Binah and Chokmah in the Tree of Life, they are on the same vibrational layer but on opposed sides of the universal scale. That is in tune with the antagonistic forces of the archetypical Scorpion and Scarab as learned in the Asetian tradition. However, each sephirah, just like any subtle object of creation, embodies duality within itself. As an example of such reality, the sephirah of Binah, being the highest manifestation of the divine feminine in the Tree of Life, has a double face. It is at the same time the holy virgin and the intoxicating sexual beast: a violent expression of the *Sexual Flame* in its purest and most divine form.

At this point it becomes relevant to explain that masculine and feminine principles, as well as energy polarities, are independent of biological sexuality. This means that an incarnated stage through the Left Pillar of the Scorpion does not imply an incarnated female, just like a spiritual state attuned within the Right Pillar of the Scarab does not embody a strictly masculine principle. The Kabbalistic glyph hides a vast world of knowledge condensed in a limited group of shapes and symbols. As a further example on the level of complexity when studying the Tree of Life we have the sephirah Netzach that in terms of astrology is connected with the planet Venus, which is often associated with the symbolism of the woman; however, in here it is rightfully located in the column of the Right Pillar, which embodies a masculine foundation. The interpretations drawn from this magickal device are immense and its study should never be approached lightly.

An Asetian, just like each individual student of Asetianism, can walk through the different initiatory paths of the Tree and attain the level of consciousness embodied in each sephirah. Just because the three sephiroth of the Left Pillar are associated with the archetypical nature of the Scorpion that does not mean that a Scarab or a Serpent will not walk that same path; on the contrary, as the Tree of Life is universal and its initiatory framework is meant to be experienced in full. Each individual Asetian is unique and the Family is expressed through diversity. The Lineages are not meant to be interpreted as categorizations of the soul, since such an attempt would be both impossible and futile.

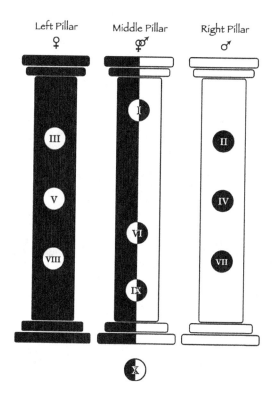

In terms of astronomy and astrology the sephiroth are also used to represent the solar system, where each individual sphere embodies the energy and influence of a specific planet or celestial body. Malkuth as expected represents the Earth itself, while Yesod is the Moon and Tiphareth the Sun, both powerful astronomical influences located in the Middle Pillar. Hod embodies Mercury, Netzach Venus, Geburah

Mars, Chesed Jupiter, Binah Saturn, Chokmah Neptune and finally, Kether represents Pluto, the most inaccessible and outer body in the solar system, just like Kether in the soul. You may have noticed the absence of Uranus in my description and that is because it is actually represented by the Abyss itself and it is embodied by the false and invisible sephirah of Da'ath.

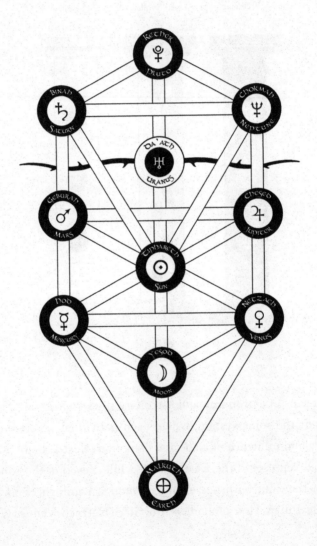

There is no mere coincidence that below the Abyss where the manifest reality is located we have seven, and specifically seven, sephiroth. That is the realm below the Duat, governed by the seven universal keys of mystery. Intimately related with the Asetian tradition and extensively explored in its many layers of Egyptian magick, seven is a very special and sacred number due to a complexity of reasons, but one in particular is the *Seven Sacred Pillars* of Asetianism.[6]

Ankh. Khepri. Ka. Tiet. Was. Ba. Ib.

These are the cosmic forces and hidden keys that sustain the manifest Universe and give it meaning; the foundations that comprise the microcosm and macrocosm that exist inside each one of us. The reason why I continuously describe these keys as *hidden* is due to their profound initiatory nature and the realization that their proper understanding can open spiritual doors that are able to reach deeper than the wisdom found in any religion or dogma, and because such mysteries cannot be fully understood through any form of literature, painting or music, but only by looking within and gazing into the stars.

"When you look long into an abyss, the abyss looks into you."
Friedrich Nietzsche

The Tree of Life presents its students with three trinity units above the mundane existence in a triple process that generates three emanations. Again, the initiatory nature of *three* is revealed. For Asetianists it now becomes clear how the Tree represents the essence of the Lineages and their triple nature, from a divine and pure emanation beyond the gates of the Duat into their earthly manifestation while incarnated in the realm of flesh. It mirrors the process of reincarnation as well as the ascension to enlightenment, so always remember that the paths work both up and down the Tree. To an initiate of the Asetian tradition this study reveals a very special key, where the inscrutable, indefinable and timeless veil of the highest manifestation of divinity that the Kabbalistic scholars have described as Ain Soph can in fact be *simply* approached as a philosophical representation of Aset...

Tetragrammaton

The ancient Kabbalist mystics believed reality to be divided into four distinctive worlds: Atziluth, the world of emanation; Briah, the creative world; Yetzirah, the intellectual world; and Assiah, the world of matter. This fourfold division of the Universe echoes the deeper Hebrew understanding of the Tetragrammaton יהוה. Each letter of the Tetragrammaton, Yod He Vav He, represents one Kabbalistic world.

The fourfold division of reality is meant to potentiate the study of thought and practical magick alongside the understanding of the layers of the soul; it describes manifestation and organizes its major conceptual foundations so that conscious and rational thought may be able to examine its elements through their spiritual signature. These four worlds are perfectly mirrored in the Tree of Life and represented by each of the three triads of sephiroth that developed from the higher realm of infinity, with the singular exception found in the world of Assiah, the material plane, where only one sephirah is present - Malkuth.

Each world found in Asetianism and the Kabbalah is also associated with a governing elemental, connecting the Tree of Life

✝

with the principles of alchemical practice: Fire, Water, Air and Earth. Fire governs the realm of purest energy and power; Water rules the astral land of emotion; Air empowers the layer of thought; and Earth holds dominion over the physical land of matter. As everything is so intimately connected this leads to an obvious relationship with the four suits of the Tarot, known for being archetypical embodiments of each alchemical element: Wands, pure expressions of spirit and the subtle; Cups, associated with feelings and emotions; Swords, principles of the mind and intellectual process; and Disks, related with the body, matter and the mundane.

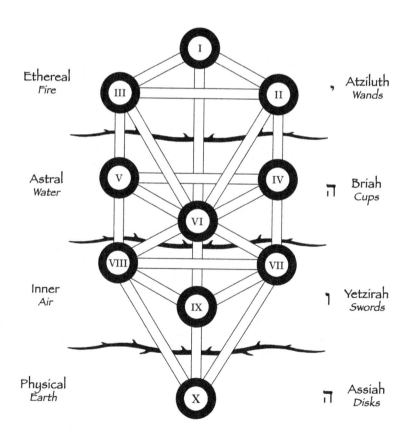

Atziluth represents the world where Kether, Chokmah and Binah live; the Yod ' of the Tetragrammaton as the land of elemental Fire, connected with the suit of Wands in the Tarot. Its Hebrew name means the land of emanations and, although it is probably the truest and most real world in the spiritual realm, it is also the harder - if not truly impossible - to understand while incarnated in a physical body. The three sephiroth present in this realm are separated from the rest of reality by a veil known as the Abyss. Being above the cloak of Da'ath means that they are still in the realm of the Duat, retaining their divine essence without distortion, and although not true deities in principle they can be approached philosophically as demigods, since the three sephirotic thrones when united as one and projected into the realm of nothingness - Ain Soph or Aset - form the unspeakable existence that is the essence of pure divinity.

Chesed, Geburah and Tiphareth are located in Briah, which the Hebrews associated with the He ה in the Tetragrammaton, the realm where elemental Water governs its power and is manifested through symbol by the suit of Cups in the Tarot. This is the land of pure emotion and creation, where the manifestation of a Higher Self presides; it is also the astral plane and in the scope of spiritual evolution it may give even the wisest seeker a feeling of representing the highest realm in existence, unaware of the reality above the Abyss.

The realm of Yetzirah holds the sephiroth Netzach, Hod and Yesod, being the final subtle reality before the world of matter; it is the Vav ו of the Tetragrammaton and manifests the powers of elemental Air, being represented in the Tarot by the suit of Swords. Here lies the formative world of inner reality: the chaotic land of the mind, thought and intricate psychology. It is also the spiritual location for the unconscious mind, the realm of dreams, wicked monsters and hidden desires. In terms of magickal practice the sephirah Hod is related to ritual and the harnessing of energy is driven from the intellect and through the mastery of wisdom, while Netzach connects with the energy drawn from music, painting and other forms of art as the path to overcome limitations. This is the lowest subtle plane, hence being often a realm of confusion, insecurity and the throne of ego. For the unbalanced mind, their own inner realm of Netzach may deceptively seem to represent the highest ladder in the spiritual world - a clear illusion driven from the lack of awareness and growth that sometimes can explain the psychology behind egocentric mindsets and ego-driven personalities.

Finally we reach the material plane of Assiah: land of Malkuth - the Kingdom. Representing the last He ה of the Tetragrammaton it naturally embodies the elemental qualities of Earth and it is present in the Tarot by the suit of Disks; the master of the physical. Assiah expresses the ultimate realm of unawareness - the very beginning of the spiritual journey. It is an impermanent road of passage in the overall path of Life, but yet an essential step to enlightenment.

In advanced studies the initiate learns to think and visualize not only in the traditional three-dimensional view but also to walk the Tree of Life in four actual dimensions. At this level of knowledge the glyph can be examined as four different expressions of the full Tree of Life in a four-dimensional world of spiritual abstraction. Although holding implications in ritual and initiatory meditations, this approach also allows for the accurate representation of the suit cards from the traditional Tarot in the Tree, as each card is connected with the sephirah under the same number and placed in one of the four Trees related to its suit. For example the *Three of Cups* card would be positioned in the third sephirah - Binah - in the Tree of Briah, regent of the element of Water. At this stage the reader that is new to the

Kabbalah or to the advanced usage of the Tarot should not worry about the fourfold system of Kabbalistic notation if it seems confusing under a first approach, as its details and considerations are only necessary in more intricate explorations and in particular when the Tree is used in tune with the archetypical system of the Tarot to map out reality and the spiritual realm.

To the initiated occultist venturing the colored pathways of the universal Tree of Life it is of extreme importance to exercise cautious diligence and to do so with courage and without hesitation, but also with awareness for the many dangers that lie in those magickal alleys and hide behind the closed doors present in its paths. The Tree when explored within advanced meditation and ritual becomes a serious magickal map that should not be treaded lightly. Although most unaware students may be protected by ignorance, lacking the keys to open the invisible gates that can lead to the most dangerous paths within the Tree, limited progress can still be attained by perseverance making the Tree of Life a stern esoteric tool that should only be used in astral charting and spiritual navigation by those with a high level of experience in the occult arts. Notwithstanding the fact that the irresponsible occultist is likely to lack the understanding and mastery to work with the most advanced forms of magick, hence rendering most of its metaphysical operations as harmless, some elemental powers may still be manifested without conscious control even if not properly wielded, making exploratory occultism an unpredictable form of magickal practice with disregard for the wisdom of esoteric arts that may produce unexpected results - often of negligible danger, but not always.

In the process of exploring the Tree, not by meditative contemplation but through the ethereal magick crafted by the ancients, the initiate shall encounter puzzles that demand solving,

†

tests that must be mastered, entities that need banishing, powers that require binding and keys that must be provided to the guardians so that you may conquer a trusted ally instead of awakening a monster. The ancient masters entrusted this warning to their apprentices, so that the curious seekers may be aware that while the lower paths of the cosmos may appear to be inviting, vulnerable and even safe, some of the most experienced occultists exploring the intricate paths leading to the higher temples have been lost forever.

The multiple warnings of peril and danger found in any serious order, coven or group studying the Kabbalah and the traditional restrictions imposed on this path of learning along with its implied veil of secrecy, as maintained since the ancient times of the early Kabbalistic rabbis, are not practical implications driven from a desire to maintain an elitist form of enlightenment, but actually a thoughtful mechanism to protect the initiate venturing through this dangerous realm of wisdom.[7]

All this information and relationships between concepts may seem like a world of knowledge to process at once if the initiate is not yet familiar with the terminology and philosophy under study, so rereading and further examination of this book is advisable as well as taking benefit from recurring reference to the material being presented. As a note, and in the scope of scholarly completion, it should also be referenced that some schools of thought have adopted a different organization of the sephiroth into the four Kabbalistic worlds, like for example the usage of Kether as the sole representation of Atziluth, with Chokmah and Binah manifesting Briah and the six non-materialistic sephiroth below the Abyss being included in Yetzirah, retaining Malktuh alone in Assiah. There is no requirement to study the other systems in order to understand the Tree of Life and they are only mentioned in this context so that the student is given awareness of their existence. Although no approach should be labeled as entirely inaccurate, since they develop from contrasting angles and express different usages, it is important to be aware of those differences when studying the published literature on the Kabbalah as it is common for the seeker to come into contact with the different systems that without said mention and awareness of their existence, often neglected by the authors, could lead to much confusion.

It becomes relevant to remind that the Kabbalistic system, in particular the exploration and understanding of the Tree of Life, is an initiatory form of wisdom where information is often withheld and intentionally altered in publication by initiated authors with the intent to protect some of the most powerful esoteric keys from the preying eyes of non-adepts. However, in this case we have adopted a clear, concise and accurate representation of the system as studied within the Aset Ka in order to avoid confusion and misrepresentation of something that is already inherently complex by nature. Although this openness and revealing of otherwise secret material represents a conscious choice that will be contested and disapproved by initiates of the mysteries and other esoteric societies, I must state as the author of this grimoire that we are not governed by outside occult policy, in any form, when determined by other Orders or bound to the vows of secrecy in them established except our own.

Having made this clear, we may continue this examination of Kabbalistic wisdom as it now becomes comprehensible how the worlds found in the Tree of Life have an almost direct correspondence with the planes of existence studied in Asetianism and discussed in further detail within the Asetian Bible - the Physical, Inner, Astral, Ethereal and Divine. However, in Asetianism you have studied five universal planes and in the Kabbalah there are only four worlds of manifestation.

This apparent difference is inexistent under a closer look, as the plane defined in the Asetian tradition as the Divine - the infinite indefinable reality beyond all creation - is expressed in Kabbalistic thought as the concept of Ain Soph; the inscrutable world beyond thought.

This fifth world is not always seen as a true plane of existence because it is actually the expression of infinity and not a proper reality defined by boundary or concept - it is the indefinable All.

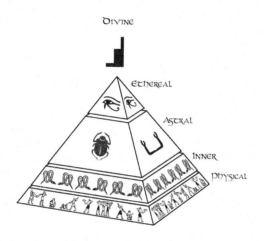

Although the four worlds - or five, depending on how you visualize it - represent the full reality of body, mind, energy and spirit, the two lower planes - Assiah and Yetzirah - are the ones most people would be familiar with and recognize under spiritual practice, being mostly unaware of the other two realms above, which are in fact far more real, permanent and eternal than the lower realities they may perceive as their full existence.

This realization on the existence and spiritual quality of the other planes can be considered a small initiation per se, as awareness and study of those realities already opens the potential doors for their exploration.

✝

Tarot

While addressing the intricate world of Tarot symbolism I would like to start by establishing that the Asetian approach to this occult art is highly spiritual, esoteric and meditative, holding no relation to the superficial and extensively proliferated side of the practice.

The Tarot should be approached as an elaborate, delicate and detailed magickal device that takes wisdom, practice and effort to master, being far more complex and deceiving than the idea perpetuated by popular culture and, as such, deserving of proper respect.

This brief chapter serves the purpose of introducing the reader to the deep spiritual connection that exists between the symbolism of the Tarot, Asetian philosophy and the wisdom of the Kabbalah. The study of the Tarot is a serious spiritual pursuit that requires years of commitment, experience and development, but one that can certainly manifest into a highly rewarding experience to the initiate. It should also be stated that the embrace and study of this occult field of symbolism and archetypical language cannot be governed by time, as learning is a continuous process and the seeker should find new lessons hidden in the cards even after years of practice. It is of paramount understanding to realize that the core of Tarot initiation is through the path of experience. Practice is vital and the key to the understanding of this art, as nothing can truly replace meditation and contemplation of the symbolism found in each individual card and the wisdom to be drawn from such magickal exploration.

To the occultist nurturing a passion for symbolism and art while collecting Tarot decks, the spiritual exploration of every new set of cards along with the meditation and study of each Arcanum is a beautiful process of self-discovery. In every deck, carefully selected to integrate the personal occult collection of the initiate, hides a world of power waiting to be written by the ink of thought and magick; a whole mystical realm to be held in your hand, explored in your meditation and conquered in your dreams.

When holding, shuffling and examining a deck of Tarot cards you should remind yourself that you are holding the keys to the mysteries of the Universe in your hands - quite literally. The Tarot as a magickal device can echo the foundations of nature, time and life through the encoded language of symbolism. It is not a mere tool to predict the future as that remains an open book waiting to be written by each of you, where every individual holds the power to craft and define his own destiny. At best, and when properly understood, the Tarot may unfold the subtle influences and universal alignments of the ethereal threads that comprise the full timeless cord of your individual lifeline, allowing for the experienced practitioner to interpret a possible or predictable future. Still, that *future* is not set in stone and surely wasn't written by the Gods, as every possible future can still be changed and remains to be written through our actions, choices and committed Will. It is important to exercise responsibility and to understand that life has no *undo* button, so every choice we make causes change in the world around us, like ripples in the fluid pond of Life. Having said that, at the Aset Ka we make a conscious effort to set our practices with the Tarot and the study of its esoteric symbolism away from the whole fortunetelling aura found in popular practice and pursued by the seekers who lack a deeper understanding of this beautiful art.

Due to the obscure initiatory nature of the Tarot and, most of all, its common misinterpretation and misrepresentation, the new age movement has seen the surging of new decks and designs spreading like a wild virus of occult ignorance.

The illustrated art present in the vast majority of these modern decks lack the esoteric wisdom and initiatory symbolism required for a Tarot deck to function as a magickal device. These new versions tend to copy the basic symbolism and structure from older traditional decks and interpret it under a modern view, but since some authors and the companies publishing them are not fluent in the symbolical language of the Tarot and its original connection with the Kabbalah, the most subtle - but absolutely vital - details are missed. It represents another echo of a money-driven society where literally anyone can publish their own decks, as long as it is commercially viable, independently of historical and magickal accuracy and that, unfortunately, results in the mainstream exposure to the Tarot becoming polluted with shallow attempts at producing relevant occult material and the silly variations of the Arcana with demons, angels, dragons and faeries, along with other unrelated fantasy.

Although some examples are quite beautiful in terms of visual arts and the included illustrations, by lacking occult sustenance or even a basic understanding of the hidden spiritual symbolism present in the cards, those decks are rendered entirely useless to any serious occultist, particularly to those interested in its initiatory properties. Such situation has often undermined the credibility of the Tarot as a valuable field within the occult due to the esoteric illegitimacy of many works and the popular approach to the art of symbolism.

From the Tarot decks available to the general public, the two most commonly used in occult practice, and thoroughly examined within the contemporary mystery schools, are the *Rider Waite Smith* deck, developed by Arthur Edward Waite and Pamela Colman Smith, both members of the Hermetic Order of the Golden Dawn, and the *Thoth Tarot* deck, developed by Aleister Crowley and Frieda Harris. Both decks, although vastly different in their approach to art, feature the important symbolism and Kabbalistic wisdom that define them as such relevant instruments to students of the mysteries. The first deck presents a more traditional and simplistic approach, while the latter is imbued with an impressive wealth of symbolism, developed with an increased focus placed on initiation. There are other valuable Tarots available, but these two are among the most well-crafted and extensively studied cards from the publicly available decks, as well as representing one of the most respected tools used in practice throughout different occult traditions, systems and orders. Of course, there are also special initiatory decks developed within different occult orders, but those are often kept private and secret, traditionally only accessible to the initiates of each path as they reflect the nature, symbolism and culture that embodies each tradition that created them.

What all these decks - initiatory or not - should have in common, even the useless commercial ones, is featuring a set of twenty-two cards at the core of their teachings. These unique cards are commonly known as trumps, but in proper esoteric terminology they should be called *Major Arcana*. The word *Arcana* has its roots in the Latin and it means *Secrets*, so the definition of *Major Arcana* actually means *Greater Secrets*, being *Arcanum* the singular form meaning *Secret*. That is quite appropriate, as each card holds a very profound initiatory secret. The twenty-two cards of the Major Arcana express universal steps of initiation in the universal ladder of spiritual evolution that every student undergoes in his mystical quest throughout life - usually lifetimes.

Prominent English occultist Aleister Crowley called *Atus of Tahuti* - an alternative spelling for *Djehuty* - to these twenty-two cards, since it was his belief that the word *Atu* meant *Key* in Ancient Egyptian, literally designating the Major Arcana as the *Keys of Thoth*.[8]

Referring back to the wisdom of the Kabbalah previously learned throughout this *Liber*, the number of Major Arcana present in a full deck of Tarot is the same as the number of letters found in the Hebrew alphabet. Every letter should be approached as a small sigil that is connected to a specific card of the Major Arcana set, as each individual Hebrew character expresses a *secret* or, in other words, each letter connects to an initiatory path that unveils a fundamental key to the mysteries. Those secrets are hidden within the Tarot cards - as with the very nature of initiation, they are sometimes hidden in plain sight - and you can find them properly represented in the Tree of Life by the paths of wisdom that connect each sephirah in the system. The study and exploration of both magickal devices in synchrony - the Tarot and the Tree of Life - can provide the initiate with a powerful understanding to many of their esoteric questions and with the details that comprise the architecture of the Universe while manifested through spiritual creation.

Alongside the twenty-two Major Arcana - the major initiations - a full deck of Tarot includes additional fifty-six cards known as the Minor Arcana, or the *Lesser Secrets*. These cards are further organized into two distinctive categories - the court cards and the four suits.

The court cards represent the spiritual expressions of royalty and in traditional occult studies are considered to be entity-related. There are four court cards in each suit and they manifest differently in each deck. In the *Rider Waite Smith*, for example, the King, Queen, Knight and Page form the court cards; while in the *Thoth Tarot* the court set was updated to the Knight, Queen, Prince and Princess, as Crowley believed that these symbolical concepts illustrated a better embodiment of the archetypes these cards are intended to represent. In essence, both systems were developed from the Kabbalah so they can be used in practice with similar results if the underlying symbology and mystical layers are properly understood.

The four suits of the Tarot represent, quite obviously, the four elements of spiritual alchemy and they are divided into Wands, Cups, Swords and Disks (or Pentacles). As you learned through the study of this *Liber*, the Tetragrammaton יהוה can only be understood through a fourfold reality, which the Kabbalists connect with the four elemental powers that manifest the whole Universe. In occult study and alchemical symbolism Wands are known to represent the element of Fire, Cups to represent Water, Swords to represent Air and Disks to represent Earth, the lowest elemental plane of matter. If the initiate seeks to study each element through the metaphysical framework of the Asetian planes of existence, then Wands and Fire connect with the Ethereal reality, exclusive to energy and the realm of spirit, accessible only through True Will; Cups and Water are connected with the Astral plane, empowered by our passions and emotions in their purest form; Swords and Air connect with the Inner plane, controlled by our thoughts and ruled by our mind; and finally Disks and Earth are connected with the expressions from the Physical plane as archetypes of matter, health and body. Such analysis and exploration of each elemental force alongside its relationship with the planes described in the Asetian tradition sheds some enlightening light on the scope of interpretations drawn in the usage of traditional Tarot meditations and spreads.

Delving deeper into the mystical realm of the suit cards the initiate observes that each of the four suits is formed - made manifest - by a set of four court cards and additional ten numbered cards: Ace, Two, Three, Four, Five, Six, Seven, Eight, Nine and Ten. These last - but certainly not least - ten suit cards are expressions of the sephiroth present in the Tree of Life, starting by the energy in its purest form through the Aces in Kether and going down the whole Tree through its ten emanations, ending in the most material and unaware form with the Tens in Malkuth. Looking at the number of each sephirah in the representation of the Tree, we find its corresponding numbered card from the Minor Arcana of the Tarot: perfect synchrony.

This realization further develops on the notion that a deeper study of the Kabbalah is at the foundation of any occultist wishing to venture into the symbolical world of the Tarot. Its connections are tremendous and they provide many of the keys to the hidden meanings, initiations and wisdom lost in this forgotten art: one that so many fail to acknowledge, let alone comprehend. The serious study and understanding of both occult fields - the Tarot and the Kabbalah - also provide the required symbolical language to understand many contemporary esoteric works. A classical example is the apparently daunting complexity of Aleister Crowley's *The Book of the Law*, as it is largely developed on the unification of symbolism and concepts from the Kabbalah and the Tarot.

> *"Invoke me under my stars! Love is the law, love under will. Nor let the fools mistake love; for there are love and love. There is the dove, and there is the serpent. Choose ye well! He, my prophet, hath chosen, knowing the law of the fortress, and the great mystery of the House of God. All these old letters of my Book are aright; but צ is not the Star. This also is secret: my prophet shall reveal it to the wise."*

AL I:57[9]

This is one of the several passages where said connections become more perceptible as the *Book* being mentioned is in fact the full deck of the Tarot, the *Star* is Major Arcanum XVII and the *fortress* is Major Arcanum XVI, The Tower; while צ is naturally the letter Tsadi of the Hebrew alphabet, determining the positioning of the archetype

✝

found in a Major Arcanum in its specific path of initiation in the Tree of Life.

After years of adaptation and mingling with popular culture the Tarot remains an esoteric art of nameless origin as, although scholars arguably trace its introduction into Europe from Mamluk Egypt, historians still struggle to locate its earlier development, but the wisdom translated in the cards by the means of symbolism is universal and can be found all around us, from the most secretive occult traditions to common objects of no particular value as modern playing cards, where the Wands became Clubs, Cups became Hearts, Swords became Spades and Disks became Diamonds. The arcane symbolism and spiritual interpretation may seem *lost* but its hidden wisdom remains unchanged, only to be unveiled by those who are able to see what lies hidden in plain sight...

✝

Liber Sigillum 333

*S*igillum 333 is a composite magickal seal or sigil created within the Order of Aset Ka, which embodies the spiritual mysteries of Orion and is used by the initiates of the Asetian tradition in meditation, ritual, initiation and esoteric study.

The word *Orion* has its roots in the Latin and is found in the Greek mythology as the expression of the divine hunter, placed by Zeus among the stars. Dating several centuries prior to the birth of Christ, the oldest works of Greek literature, such as Homer's poems in *The Iliad*, make references to Orion and describe the star Sirius as his loyal dog. A celebration to Orion was held at the city of Tanagra, in Greece, as late as the Roman Empire. It does not take much effort to realize how the concept has developed from earlier Egyptian myths - where most Greek mythology and wisdom originated - as the *hunter* is in fact a representation of the *universal predator*. Although the Greek tale of Orion eventually developed in an entirely different fashion of no particular spiritual interest, its underlying origins in the wisdom of Kemet are there, hidden in plain sight.

In Ancient Egypt the constellation of Orion was known as *Sah* and its spiritual significance was of central importance in the initiatory mysteries of its priesthood and in the interpretation of the cycles of Life and Death, as it is found in the older funerary texts.[10]

The word *Sah*, sometimes thought to represent a deity but illustrating a spiritual concept more akin to the personification of an initiatory path and layer of power rather than an embodiment of a specific divinity, was considered magickal and used in ancient spells, prayers and ritualistic utterances. The word alone is a magickal mantra that holds mystical power when uttered in proper practice, a secret the ancients have written in the stars.

Many centuries after the Orion mysteries developed in Ancient Egypt, the Christian Bible mentions Orion specifically three times in its passages, often in a cryptic way, serving as a reminder that the old secrets have not been forgotten. In Chinese astronomy Orion was known as *Shen* 参[11][12] - a character connected with a healing herb used in Traditional Chinese Medicine - where coincidentally the spelling of *Shen* is also the transliteration of an important Ancient Egyptian word and hieroglyph related with the concept of infinity and used in the Asetian tradition to describe the energy centers of the soul in the field of subtle anatomy.[13] In modern literature a reference to Orion was also not forgotten by renowned English scholar and writer J.R.R. Tolkien in his epic literary work *The Lord of the Rings*, where the Orion constellation was described by the Elves as *Menelvagor*, a Sindarin name appropriately meaning the *Swordsman of the Sky*. In Tolkien's mythology the stars of Orion were drawn in the sky of Middle Earth by Elbereth - also known as Varda, meaning *Star Lady* - who in the ancient days empowered the stars with secrets to watch and guard from the sky.[14][15]

Orion is an astronomical constellation stretching along the celestial equator and visible across the globe, which in initiatory occult studies represents a naturally formed sigil composed by seven major stars. This sigil unfolds the philosophical thread to many important spiritual mysteries, but primarily holds the key for the secrets of Death, Life and Rebirth in its triple formula as examined in this work. The core of the sigil is formed by a recognizable asterism - an astronomical pattern of stars - known as the *Belt of Orion*, and it is formed by the stars Alnitak or Zeta ζ Orionis, Alnilam or Epsilon ε Orionis and Mintaka or Delta δ Orionis.

Recent astronomical research suggests that Alnitak is located at roughly 800 light years away from the Earth and it shines 100000 times stronger than the Sun; Alnilam is 375000 times more luminous than the Sun and is located over 1300 light years away from the Earth; while Mintaka, distanced from our planet by around 900 light years has a light 90000 times brighter than the Sun.[16][17]

Inside the constellation of Orion and below the three mentioned stars there is an area described in mythology as the *Sword of the Hunter* - the tool of the predator. This interstellar object, believed by the ancients to be another star, is in fact a far more complex structure known as a nebula. The Orion Nebula looks like an inspiring work of art created by the Gods, carved ethereally in the dark sky in shades of violet and red. Located below the triple belt, as mentioned in the book's introduction, this beautiful and mysterious cosmic panting is a place for the birth of stars, holding a wealth of significance for science, philosophy and spirituality.

The natural sigil is completed with other four major stars that encircle the central three present in the Belt of Orion, and they are Bellatrix, Betelgeuse, Saiph and Rigel, the brightest star in the constellation. Together with the three stars at the core of the sigil they form a magickal symbol composed of seven stars. The numbers *three* and *seven* are nothing new in respect to their power and spiritual significance to anyone fluent in the symbolism of the Aset Ka. This natural sigil of Orion drawn in the sky by the forces of the cosmos constitutes the centerpiece of *Sigillum 333*, to be examined in detail along the following pages, and it is sometimes designated as *The Inner Sigil* in advanced studies of this powerful composite seal.

For those seeking the knowledge of initiation and enlightenment through Asetianism it becomes important to realize and accept how this tradition can work as a magickal mirror that the student must learn to study and observe; one that will sometimes reflect and even augment your own flaws so that you can find your true nature without being able to hide behind a socially crafted mask.

Once the initiate breaks free from all forms of limitation and conditioning - imposed by others but also raised by Self - the Asetian path will only reveal pure reality, expressed by the often hidden but profoundly revelatory inner truth, whether or not he is willing to accept it.

Every spiritual and metaphysical initiation within the Asetian magickal system is permanent and irreversible so this document is hereby presented with a word of caution. Responsibility is an essential prerequisite in the study of any advanced magickal tradition, but even more sternly relevant in the case of Asetian spirituality. The very transformational nature of Asetian magick, philosophy and psychology make the spiritual practice found within this tradition a considerably dangerous system if not approached with maturity and respect, particularly when dealing with material that is actively used in initiation. The subtle seed of Asetianism can only be planted deep into the rich soil of the soul. If allowed to germinate, no matter if the initiate is a long time expert in the Asetian magickal arts and wisdom or simply a young inexperienced but hungry student, that seed will sprout its divine fruits of enlightenment in the most adequate way to the seeker's reality and spiritual context. That Asetian sparkle, a subtle mark carved within your soul, will grow and live with you forever as a silent beacon of violet light; a perpetual reminder that the Asetians are still here and their magick lingers in the simpler things in nature.

A Word on Initiation

The ability to see, interpret and understand the mysteries that lie hidden in plain sight is what we designate by an *initiation*. The concept of initiation is one of the most misunderstood in occult studies, sometimes even exploited by those that do not understand the true nature of initiatory magick. In simple terms someone initiated - and this applies to all mystery schools and occult societies worthy of their name - refers to an individual that is able to see what others cannot. This does not necessarily imply that through initiation someone must develop any sort of supernatural power that would turn him into something greater than the surrounding unaware population. It simply means that they are the ones who were taught the hidden keys - the mystery - that would provide them with the knowledge to see what is hidden in plain sight. Quite simple... But also quite sophisticated. It may be seen as a road for the becoming of greatness, but such power comes from understanding and the subtle truth found within, not by an exercise of mystical power.

Using a very simple example, if you visit an old Christian church in Europe with a friend who has never studied the occult and notice a pentagram engraved on its stone walls - and it would not be as rare of a find as you might think - you immediately make the connection that at some point in history that church and its founders probably had a secretive connection with traditional witchcraft found in old Europe or with alchemy and earlier pagan practices. Depending on the surrounding symbolism and historical background you can even draw intimate connections as to what specific tradition they might have followed and what sort of ritual practices and metaphysical beliefs they held. Your friend - here representing the uninitiated - would probably walk by the symbol and not even notice it, as his mind is not programmed or attuned to pay attention to unknown symbolism, automatically rejecting most of what is alien to their conscious symbolical code. Even if he would notice the pentagram he would most likely just discard it and ignore it.

In this case you would be the initiated, as you would have the keys to another layer of understanding that your friend wouldn't have. You would know the *mystery* of said initiation and so you would be able to see what was there, hidden in plain sight, while it would still remain *invisible* to others. That is the true nature of initiation that most occult societies have kept secret for so many centuries.

By making the readers of this *Liber* aware of this vital but often overlooked magickal concept, I will provide some very important keys to the mysteries of *Sigillum 333* and how as a ritualistic and meditative seal it gracefully succeeds in the embodiment of the Orion secret using the language of symbol, the Kabbalah, the Hebrew alphabet, sacred geometry and, of course, the Asetian path. Such details when unveiled to the student of the occult and properly studied in inner practice will provide him with the necessary knowledge to understand, interpret and further explore the sigil of Orion, as he will never look blindly to its representation ever again, now seeing in it - and through it - what others cannot; becoming initiated into its mysteries.

Initiation provides the student with the tools that allow him to develop another level of awareness - an understanding deeper than that of the mundane mind. Once initiated into the mysteries the adept experiences his world changing forever, as he is now able to see what others cannot through a newfound perception empowered by knowledge. Some may dislike you, judge you or condemn you, as they would lack the ability to see through the initiated Eyes that you now possess. There is no point in arguing or forcing understanding on an uninitiated mind, as their thoughts will not shift nor will their eyes open wide simply because they lack the key to see what you can see. It is the proper road for the initiate - and I would dare say the only wise mindset - to just ignore those that may condemn you from below and instead opt to simply bask in the renewed light of your now initiated Eyes. As I always say... use them wisely.

The occult has always been and will remain a land of deceit. That reality is a positive learning ground for initiation as it makes easier to distinguish the weak from the brave and the foolish from the wise. If the seeker does not develop a strong sense of awareness and perception from the start of his inner journey he will eventually fall into one of the many deceptive pits. Do not give up on the first time you fail to reach for the ladder of wisdom, but instead remember that strength is measured by your ability to get up and admit that you have fallen, otherwise your misstep will not take you through the veil of unspeakable abyss but rather drown you in the ocean of oblivion. That is why, when clouded in the apparent inability to accomplish their own Great Work and to grasp through the veil of the ancient mysteries, some attempt to climb the hidden steps of enlightenment by spreading a layer of deceitful self-importance instead of simply standing on their own.

At the dawn of time we remain confident in our cosmical role of silent initiators.

The Three Secrets

Three is a special magickal number. Although it is a simple mathematical element for the uninitiated, there is much magick and wisdom hidden inside, only waiting to be found, studied and liberated by the student of the mysteries.

Orion is examined in the context of this *Liber* as a spiritual expression for the mystical formulae of the sacred Three, where the central stars that form the constellation's belt - Alnitak, Alnilam and Mintaka - are at the core of these teachings. They embody a powerful expression for the spiritual archetype found in each Asetian Lineage -

Serpent, Scarab and Scorpion -, as well as the symbolical hallmark for
the three-folded path of Death, Life and Rebirth, so important to any
mystical tradition. This connection and spiritual framework is present
throughout history in many forms of occult architecture, being most
notably pioneered by the Ancient Egyptians in their religious
edifications, particularly demonstrated in the state-of-the-art
technology - in terms of science, engineering and metaphysics - found
in the iconic initiatory temples that became known as the Pyramids,
located in the necropolis of Giza.

The Pyramids of Khufu, Khafre and Menkaure are a symbolic
mirror of the sky meant to function as a metaphysical door to the
cosmos, raised among the heat and dust of the Egyptian desert. When
conceptually aligned with Orion they are a perfect expression of the
formation of the Asetian Lineages as found in the Kabbalistic Tree of
Life. The three stars high in the sky can be understood as the spiritual
emanation from the three Primordials located above the Abyss - in the
timeless realm of the Duat -, while the physical Pyramids express their
earthly manifestations below Da'ath as the incarnations from the three
distinctive Lineages reflecting their archetypes from above.

Such understanding brings further meaning to the legacy of
Thoth succinctly described by the formula *"As Above, so Below,"* which
defines one of the conceptual backbones for the architecture of Asetian
spirituality. In a Latin translation of the legendary work of Thoth
known as the *Emerald Tablet* or *Tabula Smaragdina*, which is also
included in the medieval dissertation *Secretum Secretorum* originally in
Arabic, we find the following passage:

> *"Quod est inferius est sicut quod est superius, et quod est
> superius est sicut quod est inferius, ad perpetranda
> miracula rei unius."*

☥

The sentence translates to *"That which is below is as that which is above, and that which is above is as that which is below, to perform the miracles of the one thing."*

This law of Thoth is found to be accurately expressed in the sacred land of Egypt as the three Pyramids mirror the higher reality of the stars by representing Orion and its three inner mysteries, as our microcosm is only but a reflection of the subtle macrocosm hidden above the Abyss. The mundane Self is an expression of the Higher Self and the Higher Self is an expression of the Divine Self.

To the readers paying greater attention to detail, it may have come to mind why it is that throughout the whole book I have recurrently used the words Death, Life and Rebirth in this particular order while the rest of the world refers to this cycle as Life, Death and Rebirth. This change in literary order reflects an important paradigm found in Asetian spirituality that is intimately connected with the philosophy behind this work. To a regular mindset, physical Life is the focus of spiritual reality, reflected in the traditional order of Life, Death and Rebirth. People see Life as the ultimate goal and the center of their existence, so after it naturally follows Death and then the mystical Rebirth through reincarnation, and once again back to Life. This is how the vast majority of world religions that have adopted reincarnation within their philosophies express the perpetual cycle of their spiritual reality. But not the Ancient Egyptians…

In Asetianism, the ultimate liberation is not manifested through a permanent return to Life, but instead by an immortal return to Death. The Duat - Egyptian land of the dead and underworld - is the true world of *life* to an enlightened Asetian mind: their own native realm. Life is impermanent and transitory, while Death is eternal, infinite and the cradle of immortality.

Life is a powerful school of spiritual evolution, but merely a road in the universal path of growth, while Death is the true home of the soul: the throne of the Divine Self.

From this spiritual perspective Death is actually far more real than physical Life, which in mystical terms represents a powerful deceptive illusion. As dark and morbid as this may sound at first glance, it is actually quite a positive and enlightening view of the spiritual roadmap of the soul. Just like with the advanced Ancient Egyptian mind, the focus is instead placed on Death and its hidden mysteries; the breaking from the conditioning of matter and flesh to focus on the truth found within as the only real part that can survive physical death. This leads not to a sad or depressive view of the world, but actually to an enlightened mindset that has learned to enjoy life to its fullest by acknowledging its impermanent beauty and to value every moment.

With this secret in mind I have used Death, Life and Rebirth as an initiatory literary detail hidden throughout this book, since the Asetians approach the spiritual cycle with Death as their home, Life as the impermanent path in-between and Rebirth as the awakening into Death and the divine communion with Aset.

> *"Live as if you were to die tomorrow. Learn as if you were to live forever."*
>
> Mahatma Gandhi

The possible meanings behind the formulae of the sacred Three are endless and not restricted to the parallels drawn in this text. They are represented in the energy and symbolism of *Sigillum 333*, which as a powerful and intricate magickal device holds the keys to initiate the seeker with deeper layers of understanding of said formulae as he commits to further study and magickal work with the seal. In a small reference to the *Book of Giza*, the first work included in this three-folded grimoire, it is relevant to note that the occult document is formed by three distinctive Sebayt, while inside each Sebayt there are specifically thirty-three utterances. Nothing is random.

Beyond the multitude of meanings, the following pages will approach and describe three different layers of initiation from the formulae of the sacred Three, connected with *Sigillum 333*, and walk the initiate through the powerful spiritual work to be accomplished when studying the mysteries of Orion. As an esoteric tool imbued with energy and meaning, *Sigillum 333* will only continue to provide for those who have searched within its mysteries with honesty.

Sarcophagus of Flesh
The First Initiation

The descent of Spirit into matter is the spiritual process described in Asetianism as *From Purity to Dust*. While incarnated, the soul finds itself locked in a conceptual sarcophagus - the physical plane. The realization and awareness over this process and its spiritual implications are of vital importance in the work of initiation through the mysteries of Orion and its profound message of liberation. The philosophy behind this process can be properly understood during the study of *Liber* סוד, which includes a chapter dedicated to the development of the concept and its metaphysical correlation with the Tree of Life.

One famous tale found in Ancient Egyptian mythology that survived the test of time is the account of Seth locking Osiris inside a powerful box made of solid gold, in order to imprison him away from his powers and blessed life. This golden box represents the material world: a spiritual metaphor for the constricted life in the material plane.[18] It symbolizes the desire from Seth to keep the royal family locked in a superfluous world of lesser significance instead of roaming freely through the plane where they rightfully ruled - the realm of Energy and Spirit - which in his deviant greed he wanted for himself, along with the throne of Egypt. In this state of unawareness, locked inside a prison of shimmering gold, the mind and soul are kept ignorant of its full existence and true potential outside of that box. Self is maintained in deep sleep, like a lost dream where the whole reality seems to be restricted to those shining walls of deceptive gold. This is the realm where mankind is locked up and jailed; the blind reality of physical matter, the true expression of unawakened futility and ego. To most people, these conceptual walls of matter raised by the laws of the physical plane represent their complete vision of reality, living under the vain sleep where this is all that matters, unaware of the wide subtle world of possibility that exists beyond this cage of body and matter that makes most of what is thought to be valuable quite superfluous in the grand scheme of things.

This is one of the most basic secrets behind Sethian rule and influence as well as the dangerous reality behind their power; a mythical expression from a legacy of control and unawareness, fully manifested in the plane where they hold their highest power - the physical realm of matter where all unaware souls are imprisoned. This Sethian dominion is well mirrored in the last era - the *Djehuty of the Crocodile* - that is historically marked with the rise of religious slavery to dogma and the fear of the divine, along with an increasing focus on the decadence of material possession, while the subtle and nature suffered the consequences of modern thought, being neglected and defaced by men, owners of the strongest intellect among all animals and hence spiritually responsible to protect it.[19]

Without this initiation into a state of awareness the soul carries on a life of blindness to the beautiful, empowering and liberating spiritual reality that hides right above their heads and all around them, but which they can not see, feel or touch, leading to the generalized conviction that it simply does not exist. This spiritual blindness - the jail of the soul within matter - is not only manifested by those that do not accept their spiritual side, but also, and many times more deceitfully, by those who see themselves as spiritual and aware when in reality under the veil of truth they are locked into the lower depths of their physical tomb, living a life of absolute slavery controlled by many *masters* like wealth, youth, possession, recognition and appearance. Just because someone attempts to study the occult, professes a spiritual life or tries to come forth as a mystical mind capable of deeper thoughts, that alone does not imply any level of enlightenment, wisdom or awareness. In fact, many vain representations of Self that are found in people seeking the magickal arts are often a sad expression of ego, insecurity and delusion.

This is an important mindset of central study and meditation, a major accomplishment for an initiate of the Asetian path, as well as a hallmark that truly distinguishes an Asetian or a learned Asetianist from an unawakened mind, by being free in the deepest and most liberating form. Through this path the seeker experiences the purest and most powerful of all forms of freedom by cracking his own sarcophagus open - the initiation into awareness - and is free to explore the realm of Spirit and master the energies in full awareness of all his potential.

Once the jail of physical matter is broken it cannot be locked again. When the initiate achieves such a state of mental and spiritual freedom - empowering him to see a glimpse of the Universe through the Eyes of an Asetian - he cannot be blinded again and his awareness

✝

is then unleashed to harness the full spectrum of his inner potential. This alchemical process of spiritual evolution sustains the philosophical and metaphorical realization that most people being capable of seeing in *color* are actually only experiencing a powerful illusion. They truly can only see in shades of gray while under the illusion that such view is the full spectrum of color, hence assuming it as the whole manifestation of the rainbow. But once you have your first glimpse of sight in real color, if you are capable to look at what an Asetian can see even if only for a split second, then a whole new Universe unfolds in front of your eyes. That is true initiation... and it is eternal.

> *"Once learned the tools that allow to see from an Asetian*
> *perspective, the soul remains forever changed, unable to*
> *go blind again."*
>
> Tânia Fonseca

This first initiation of Orion is accurately represented in Major Arcanum XVI of the Tarot - The Tower. As a cataclysmic expression of supreme destruction, this card, like so many others, is greatly misunderstood. The collapsing of the strong structure that is the tower symbolizes the break from belief and dogma with the rupture of our physical prison. The process can be painful and often devastating, but it will set the initiate free from the conditioning of the mundane. It will unleash the soul and open the ways. Pure, absolute and fearless freedom awaits once the foundations of your inner tower are destroyed. Remember, from the darkest times come the deepest forms of liberation.

The concept of awakening, often referred to in Asetianism, and so intimately connected with the tradition of the vampire, holds a

✝

great spiritual correlation with this mystery that I have described as the *Sarcophagus of Flesh.*

The breaking of the sarcophagus of matter and the conquer of independence from all the mundane conditioning, through the attaining of conscious spiritual awareness, is a powerful form of magick and personal achievement that brings the power over the subtle - but more real - existence back to the hands of Self. This represents a profound form of awakening, so hidden but also so very real, being a true hallmark of vampire spirituality so often misunderstood by the uninitiated, still locked inside their own mystical prison.

It should be noted that none of this means to say that every mundane aspect should be rejected and discarded, or that life in the material plane is inherently shallow and obsolete. Quite on the contrary, as life in this realm is a unique opportunity to learn and evolve in ways that mere subtle existence would not potentiate. It is up to the individual to make a conscious choice and take active steps in order to embrace life in its full potential for spiritual learning rather than to simply waste it in the empty illusions of the superfluous. In the end, true power lives inside every single one of you. The physical world allows for the unfolding of True Will and its enlightening flame to be made manifest once purified in the higher realms of subtle existence. However, to reach such a venerable state of freedom, when you can master the physical plane in order to manifest your inner essence, you must first break from the deceptive chains of matter.

That is one of the greater mysteries behind the alchemy of the soul and why the ancient alchemists and Kabbalists see Earth as a lesser element. While describing the Hebrew language in *Liber* יסוד I have explained that the three primary letters of the mystical alphabet were Aleph א, Mem מ and Shin ש, representing the three major elements - Air, Water and Fire. Earth is intentionally not represented, as in the Kabbalah this elemental force is approached as less powerful than the other three. The reason behind this apparent omission lies precisely in the mystery that I have named the *Sarcophagus of Flesh*. Earth remains a powerful elemental, but a deceptive and controlling one that the occultist must learn to break in order to gain control over the other three; the ones that truly manifest the spiritual world.

So now you have learned the alchemical secret behind the mystical thought of the descent into matter; the fall from purity to dust. It is the realization on the condition of the soul upon reincarnation - its jail in the sarcophagus of flesh. This is the central spiritual mystery taught inside most secret societies in history, from ancient times to the modern day. That is the first initiation of Orion; the break from the agonizing tomb where the Ba lies hidden and locked away from its full potential. But as a first initiation, that is the very early step into Orion...

Mysteries Unveiled

The Second Initiation

In this chapter you are about to embark on the study and direct analysis of the symbolical elements present in *Sigillum 333*. If the reader is not familiar with actively working with this specific sigil and the study of its symbolism, it is suggested that he dedicates some time to the independent usage and exploration of the sigil in meditation and ritual prior to the reading of the following chapter. In ceremonial magick, the sigil may be reproduced by the occultist's method of choice, often illustrated by hand through paper and ink in a gentle process of creation not governed by the limitation of time. This is later to be consumed in magickal practice by the heat of the flame that, with

✝

the four elementals as your witness, shall destroy the artistic energies and manifest its encoded essence within the mind of the initiate.

The complexity of this sigil and its included symbolism is immense, so going through every aspect and correlation present in its different elements would result in a full book on its own. However, I will be guiding the reader in a structured study of its main initiatory elements and the development of the sigil through its several fundamental parts and the correlating magickal significance to be drawn for each layer of wisdom. During this examination make sure to use continuous reference to the full sigil included in the cover of this *Liber*.

Starting by the center of the magickal seal there is a representation of the seven major stars found in the astronomical constellation of Orion that form what we have previously designated by the natural sigil of Orion or inner sigil, here illustrated inside a black circle that symbolizes the sky - and the whole Universe - through its circular shape, an ancient symbol of perfection and geometrical personification of the absolute.

In the outer layer of the black universal circle there is an hexagram with six symbols differentiated into two different groups of inverted coloration - the basic hieroglyphs for the three Asetian Lineages in black with white background and three Greek letters drawn in white laying inside a black background.

The Ancient Egyptian symbols for the Lineages and their significance require no introduction to a student of Asetian magick, but the Greek letters might appear as a surprise to some. They are used in this sigil due to their scientific and historical significance in terms of astronomy, as they correlate with the three stars in the belt of Orion - ζ is the letter Zeta and symbolizes Alnitak, ε is the letter Epsilon and represents Alnilam, and δ is the letter Delta and expresses Mintaka.

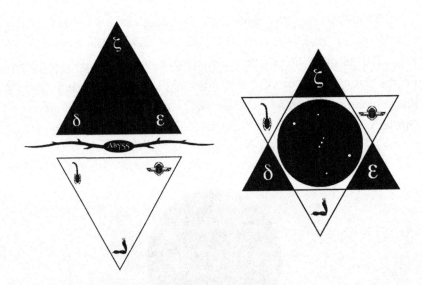

What might not be perceivable at surface is that this hexagram is in fact the union of two opposed triangles. The first one in black with the representation of the stars - the divine reality - and the second in white with the representation of the Lineages - the earthly manifestation of the higher stars below the Abyss.

When crossed together and united by the transcendence of the alchemical Abyss, they allow for the refraction of spiritual light and make visible the universal truth at the center, as expressed by the natural sigil of Orion, like two powerful magickal lenses that when placed at the top of each other by the hands of the Elders can reveal a hidden image - the secret.

As the reader should now realize, these two triangles hide the mystery of the descent into matter - *From Purity to Dust* - through the formation process of the Tree of Life as I have described in *Liber* יסוד. When the triangles - two-dimensional symbolical representations of a pyramid here illustrated in inverted position - are moved together and united they become one singular entity and define the geometrical figure known as the hexagram.

Once the hexagram is formed, the archetypes of the Lineages and their divine emanations are now facing each other as opposed smaller triangles - Alnitak and Khufu are facing the Serpent; Alnilam and Khafre are facing the Scarab and Mintaka and Menkaure are facing the Scorpion.

The learned Kabbalist can see the most transcendental realms of the Tree of Life - the world of Atziluth in black and Briah in white - accurately represented in the sigil as the two higher triads of sephiroth appear in their right positions inside the two triangles of this secret: Kether, Chokmah and Binah in black; Chesed, Geburah and Tiphareth in white. The symbolism of the sigil finds the supernal triad of the higher emanations expressed by Alnitak, Alnilam and Mintaka, and their manifest incarnations below Da'ath properly represented by the known Lineage hieroglyphs.

The hexagram being the union of two opposed triangles, one regular and another inverted, further hides another profound symbolical message. These two triangles are the traditional alchemical symbols for Fire and Water; the two major opposed forces and energies in the Universe. By combining them inside us through the magick of the seal we achieve the ultimate alchemy as the perfect union of opposites - the Hexagram: a powerful representation of balance and spiritual equilibrium.

This is the great secret behind the symbolism of the hexagram as studied within the Aset Ka, an initiatory detail that you now may understand as it remains hidden in plain sight, as a simple hexagram shall never look the same again.

Its spiritual message is profound and transformational, but once fully understood and assimilated it becomes clear and beautiful in its simplicity. This hidden meaning is also unequivocally represented in Major Arcanum XIV of the Tarot, entitled Temperance, in which its traditional design a winged figure with a triangle at the chest mixes an unknown mystical fluid between two golden goblets. This is the Tarot card that Aleister Crowley infamously altered its name to Art, generating much controversy among the uninitiated. This *Art* that he refers to is the unification of the opposed forces present in duality as the internal alchemy of the occultist, and in the redesigned version of his deck Frieda Harris has drawn a figure with two heads pouring Fire and Water into a magickal cauldron. This literally illustrates the mystical union of Fire and Water, the two alchemical elements represented by the opposed triangles that create our hexagram. The two-headed figure mingling the elementals through her magickal art signifies the perfect bond and union of the King and the Queen, but Crowley and Harris went even further in the symbolism included in the card, as this androgynous entity is controversially depicted with six breasts, which you now can see represent the six smaller triangles that form our hexagram.

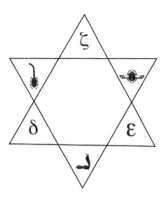

As we get deeper into the mysteries of the spiritual alchemy present in *Sigillum 333* by understanding the revealing detail that our hexagram is in fact the union of two alchemical symbols, the reader may acknowledge two smaller triangles at the top and another two below the hexagram figure inside the seal. These are the renowned alchemical symbols used in magick to represent the four elemental forces of the Universe - Fire, Water, Air and Earth. In Ancient Egyptian mythology these powerful elementals were hidden behind the theological concept of the *Four Sons of Horus,* and they were known as Imset, Qebehsenuf, Duamutef and Hapi - the four canopic jars used in the process of mummification.[20][21]

The traditional occult method of thinking and practical magick is actually an exercise of highly scientific formulae, as the tools of the alchemist and initiatory occultist, described as the four elemental powers, are accurately represented in modern science, studied in physics and chemistry as the four states of matter: solid, liquid, gas and plasma. The physical properties of solid states are akin to the metaphysical qualities of elemental Earth, just like liquid is comparable to alchemical Water, gas is related to Air and plasma naturally equates with magickal Fire.

Each of these elements in the sigil interconnects two archetypes of different Lineage, hinting at further alchemical implications between the dual emanations. They are represented between a higher and a lower emanation, never of the same Lineage. For example, the symbol for Fire is between the ζ of Alnitak connected with the divine Serpent and the incarnated Scorpion, while the symbol for Earth is located between the ε of Alnilam connected with the divine Scarab and the image of the incarnated Serpent. These complex correlations, hard to understand on a first study, are related with the potential of energy interaction between the essence from two different Lineages and how that wisdom can be used in the alchemy of the soul through highly advanced metaphysical work, while it also establishes an accurate ritualistic framework concerning the ideal process of elemental evocation in Asetian ceremonial magick.

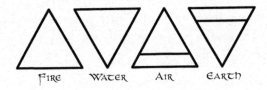

FIRE   WATER   AIR   EARTH

On each side of the hexagram there are two hieroglyphs of the Ankh ☥ - one straight and another inverted. This ancient hieroglyph is of central importance in the Ancient Egyptian tradition where it was considered sacred and often only represented in the hands of the Gods. In terms of language it translates literally to *Life* and it is related with the Asetian view of immortality. It is a powerful sigil in its own right, owner of one of the most ancient symbological legacies found in history with vast magickal and spiritual implications and, although often abused and misrepresented in modern times, its many layers of power are out of the scope of this *Liber*. The two Ankh included in this

☥

sigil convey several occult meanings, but the one we will reveal in this study is connected with *The Pillars of the Mysteries*. As you have learned in *Liber* יסוד the left side of the Tree of Life manifested by the sephiroth Binah, Geburah and Hod - different emanations of the Scorpion archetype - is known as the Left Pillar and it is a spiritual representation of our own inner darkness, here illustrated in the sigil by an inverted Ankh on the left. While visualizing the Tree of Life represented in the seal you should realize that by being positioned between the Scorpion and δ this inverted Ankh appears accurately located in Geburah and Binah.

On the right side of the Tree we have Chokmah, Chesed and Netzach as emanations of the Scarab, here illustrated by the straight Ankh; our face of light. Placed in the sigil between the Scarab and ε, the Ankh properly appears by the side of Chesed and Chokmah when visualizing the Tree of Life and its sephiroth. With this mindset, at the center of the sigil the representation of Orion through its seven-folded mysteries or stars can also be seen as a secret Ankh, symbolizing the Middle Pillar, as the balance and unification of opposite forces accurately located in symbol between ζ and the Serpent - Kether and Tiphareth - the two first sephiroth of the Middle Pillar in the Tree of Life.

The study of these connections and symbolism as it draws knowledge from different layers of wisdom and traditions may seem confusing on a first approach, hence why several readings of this document is recommended while in the process of studying the sigil, until all elements and their relevance are understood and properly assimilated.

Reaching the outer rim of the sigil the student finds a black circumference with six letters of the Hebrew alphabet. This alphabet is

☦

of central significance in every layer of knowledge related to the Kabbalah as well as extensively used in the foundation of Western mysticism for centuries. Its importance, symbolism and conceptual development can be properly understood during the study of *Liber יסוד*, where the reader can learn the secret behind the formation of the twenty-two letters that compose it. These small and curvy letter-sigils identify with each of the twenty-two initiatory paths found connecting the ten sephiroth in the Tree of Life, as well as the twenty-two Major Arcana from the traditional Tarot. With this in mind it becomes clear how each singular Hebrew letter embodies the symbolism of every spiritual pathway found in this system, so uniquely illustrated through art and color in the paintings of the Tarot cards.

In the sigil of Orion - which we described as *Sigillum 333* - the six Hebrew letters represented in the outer circle of the seal are located near the geometrical vertex of each of the individual six triangles generated by the union of alchemical Fire and Water as previously studied. Adopting a clockwise progression the selected Hebrew letters are Vav ו, Kaph כ, He ה, Beth ב, Gimel ג and Yod י. Two letters for each Lineage, in a divine and earthly manifestation of its energies. Again... duality.

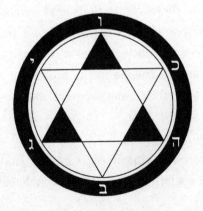

✝

Located in Alnitak ζ and the Serpent we have the letters Vav ו and Beth ב. Vav ו represents the archetype of the illuminated guide, connected with Major Arcanum V of the Tarot - The Hierophant -, an universal symbol for the inscrutable connection between the human and the divine; a link between the sacred and the profane. Beth ב as a representation of knowledge and wisdom is tied to Major Arcanum I of the Tarot - The Magus - that beneath its mystical power also holds the dangerous trap of lack of conscience.

Near Alnilam ε and the Scarab we find the letters He ה and Kaph כ. He ה is a personification of transformational energies and purification, related to Major Arcanum XVII of the Tarot - The Star - that leaves a message of hope, possibility and eternity. Kaph כ is connected with dynamism and movement, which through Major Arcanum X of the Tarot - Wheel of Fortune - hints at new beginnings, uncertainty and the roads of fate.

Connected to Mintaka δ and the Scorpion are the letters Gimel ג and Yod י. Gimel ג is a letter of profound lunar influence, associated with Major Arcanum II of the Tarot - The High Priestess - that as the initiatrix she represents an archetype of intuition, trust and delicate strength. Yod י embodies darkness and introspection through Major Arcanum IX of the Tarot - The Hermit -, a mystical view on the rejection of the mundane and the quest for inner light, sometimes also connected with isolation and solitude.

It is important to keep in mind that all these cards and their wealth of symbolism are universal spiritual archetypes that represent powerful ideas and initiations, not emotional or psychological characteristics, so they should never be interpreted lightly. Their message and meaning is profound as each represents a single Major Arcanum of the Tarot, which in Latin means *Greater Secret*, here only represented six out of the twenty-two possible paths of life once the initiate sets forth in his inner quest for enlightenment through the worlds of the Tree of Life. Once more I urge the readers to remain aware that the Tarot cards being referred to, as well as their archetypal meanings, do not represent an attempt to categorize each Lineage in whatever form but instead are used in this context as initiatory facets of the dual emanations from each Lineage and their location in the Tree of Life, particularly due to their positioning above and below the Abyss of Da'ath. To simplistically associate the mysteries of an Arcanum from the Tarot with a specific Lineage would be a mistake.

As a last detail, there are three circles of different radius and thickness featured in the sigil, a last homage to the power and symbolism hidden behind such an apparently simplistic thing... the number Three.

The final mystery and ultimate key takes us back to the very early start of this study and it lies in the shape of Orion itself, as mirrored in the night sky while enchanting the initiatory body of Nut. That is why that illustration holds the central position in this sigil imbued with the teachings of the ancients.

Beauty is found in detail and only achieved through
simplicity.

✝

Orion Key

The Third Initiation

0. Oh the void of the Fool! Through the mystery Key thy initiation cometh veiled in Three.

1. Hidden in the darkest face of Nut lies the Key to this mystery.

2. In the aphotic hours of inner clarity consume Her naked body and thou shall see!

3. The formula from Above is three equals one and one equals one plus one so that three equals seven.

4. The Splendor lives in Beauty but Beauty lives in Strength.

5. To Crown thy Self you must not seek Wisdom but awaken Understanding.

6. The Kingdom is for the weak and the blind for thou must break free from such prison.

7. His Beauty might be seductive but only in three shall the crownless see above the Abyss.

8. Three gave three and three but only then all became one.

9. The veil of time shall now be closed for this is the hour to seal it from within.

Liber Sigillum 333

Portuguese Edition

*S*igillum *333* é um sigilo mágico ou selo compósito criado na Ordem de Aset Ka que incorpora os mistérios espirituais de Orion, sendo utilizado pelos iniciados da tradição Asetiana em práticas de meditação, rituais, iniciação e estudos esotéricos.

A palavra *Orion* tem origem no Latim e encontra-se na mitologia Grega como a expressão do caçador divino, colocado por Zeus no céu entre as estrelas. Alguns séculos antes do nascimento de Cristo, poemas antigos da literatura Grega como *A Ilíada* de Homero, fazem referência a Orion e descrevem a estrela Sirius como o seu cão de confiança. Historicamente, celebrações dedicadas a Orion foram mantidas na cidade de Tanagra, na Grécia, até ao período do Império Romano. No estudo dos mistérios e legado histórico, é simples compreender como a simbologia de Orion se desenvolveu a partir de conceitos Egípcios mais antigos - onde grande parte da mitologia e conhecimento Gregos encontram a sua origem - pois o *caçador* é, na realidade, uma representação do conceito espiritual do *predador universal*. Embora a mitologia Grega em torno de Orion se tenha eventualmente desenvolvido de uma forma sem especial interesse espiritual, as suas origens no conhecimento Kemético estão bem presentes, escondidas à vista de todos.

O significado espiritual da constelação de Orion, conhecida por *Sah* no Antigo Egipto, tinha um papel de extrema importância nos mistérios iniciáticos bem como na interpretação dos ciclos da Vida e da Morte, como é comprovado pelos textos funerários mais antigos.[10] A palavra *Sah*, por vezes usada como referência a uma divindade, mas mais correctamente representativa de um conceito espiritual relacionado com a personificação de um caminho iniciático, era considerada mágica e utilizada em encantamentos antigos, orações e expressões ritualistas. A palavra em si é um mantra esotérico que esconde um ténue mas profundo poder místico quando proferida em práticas das artes ocultas, um segredo que os anciãos escreveram nas estrelas.

Vários séculos depois dos mistérios de Orion se terem desenvolvido no Antigo Egipto, a Bíblia Cristã refere Orion especificamente três vezes nas suas passagens, muitas vezes de uma forma encriptada, relembrando que os velhos segredos não foram esquecidos. Na astronomia Chinesa, a constelação de Orion é conhecida por *Shen* 参 [11] [12] - etimologicamente relacionada com uma erva medicinal utilizada em Medicina Tradicional Chinesa - onde, coincidentemente, a grafia de *Shen* representa também a transliteração de uma antiga palavra Egípcia ligada ao conceito de infinito, encontrada frequentemente na tradição Asetiana para descrever os centros energéticos da alma no estudo da anatomia subtil.[13] Na literatura moderna, a referência a Orion não foi também esquecida pelo reconhecido escritor Inglês J.R.R. Tolkien, na sua obra literária *O Senhor dos Anéi*s, onde a constelação de Orion é descrita pelo povo Élfico como *Menelvagor*, um nome Sindarin que adequadamente significa o *Guerreiro da Espada no Céu*. Na mitologia de Tolkien, as estrelas de Orion foram desenhadas no céu da Terra Média por Elbereth - também conhecida por Varda, a *Senhora das Estrelas* - que nos primórdios dos tempos escondeu nos céus segredos de aviso e protecção.[14] [15]

Orion é uma constelação astronómica que se estende pelo equador celeste, sendo visível por todo o globo. A nível ocultista, representa um sigilo cósmico natural, formado por sete estrelas principais. Este sigilo esconde uma profunda ligação filosófica a muitos mistérios espirituais mas, primariamente, detém a chave para os segredos da Morte, Vida e Renascimento na sua fórmula tripla, conforme explicado nos conteúdos deste livro. O núcleo do sigilo é formado por um reconhecido asterismo - um padrão astronómico de estrelas - chamado *Cinturão de Orion* e é formado pelas estrelas Alnitak ou Zeta ζ Orionis, Alnilam ou Epsilon ε Orionis e Mintaka ou Delta δ Orionis.

Recentes investigações na área da astronomia sugerem que Alnitak está localizada a aproximadamente 800 anos-luz da Terra e que brilha 100000 vezes mais do que o Sol; Alnilam é 375000 vezes mais luminosa do que o Sol e está localizada a mais de 1300 anos-luz da Terra; enquanto que Mintaka, distanciada do nosso planeta por aproximadamente 900 anos-luz, brilha 90000 vezes mais do que o Sol.[16][17]

No interior da constelação de Orion e na zona inferior das três estrelas anteriormente mencionadas, existe uma área do céu descrita na mitologia clássica como a *Espada do Caçador* - o instrumento do predador. Este objecto interestelar, identificado erroneamente pelos cientistas da antiguidade como outra estrela, é de facto uma estrutura muito mais complexa descrita cientificamente como uma nébula. A Nébula de Orion aparece como uma peça de arte criada pelos Deuses, esculpida etereamente no céu nocturno em tons de violeta e vermelho. Localizada abaixo do cinturão triplo, conforme mencionado na introdução do livro, esta bela e misteriosa pintura cósmica é um lugar de nascimento de estrelas, detendo uma enorme importância para a ciência, filosofia e espiritualidade.

O sigilo natural é completado por outras quatro estrelas que contornam as três centrais presentes no Cinturão de Orion. Elas são Bellatrix, Betelgeuse, Saiph e Rigel, a estrela mais brilhante da constelação. Todo o conjunto forma um poderoso símbolo mágico constituído por sete estrelas. Os números *três* e *sete* não representam algo novo no que diz respeito ao seu poder e significado espiritual para alguém fluente no simbolismo da Aset Ka. Este sigilo natural desenhado no céu pelas forças do Universo, também designado por *Sigilo Interior* em estudos mais avançados deste poderoso selo mágico, constitui a peça central do *Sigillum 333*, que será examinado em detalhe ao longo das próximas páginas.

Para quem procura o conhecimento de iniciação e iluminação através do Asetianismo, torna-se importante compreender e aceitar como esta tradição pode por vezes funcionar como um espelho esotérico, que o aprendiz deve aprender a estudar e a observar. Esse espelho poderá, eventualmente, reflectir e até aumentar as suas falhas e fraquezas, de forma a conseguir encontrar a sua verdadeira natureza sem lhe permitir esconder-se atrás de máscaras nem render-se ao condicionalismo das supérfluas expectativas sociais. A partir do momento em que o iniciado se liberta de tudo o que o limita e condiciona - não só imposto pelos que o rodeiam mas também por si mesmo - o caminho Asetiano irá apenas revelar a realidade mais pura, manifestada pela frequentemente escondida e obscura verdade interior mas profundamente reveladora, quer o iniciado esteja disposto a aceitá-la ou não.

Qualquer variante de iniciação espiritual ou metafísica utilizada no sistema Asetiano é permanente e irreversível e por isso este documento esotérico é aqui apresentado com uma palavra de precaução. Responsabilidade é um pré-requisito essencial no estudo de qualquer tradição mágica avançada, mas ainda mais severamente relevante no caso da espiritualidade Asetiana e das práticas metafísicas desenvolvidas neste sistema. A natureza transformacional da magia, filosofia e psicologia Asetianas, faz da prática espiritual abordada no seio desta tradição um sistema consideravelmente perigoso quando não encarado com maturidade e respeito, particularmente no caso de material usado activamente em iniciação. A semente subtil do Asetianismo só pode ser plantada no solo mais profundo e puro da alma. Se deixada germinar, quer o estudante possua um conhecimento avançado das artes Asetianas ou seja apenas um jovem iniciado e inexperiente mas ansioso por aprender, essa mesma semente vai dar origem aos frutos divinos da iluminação e sabedoria da forma mais adequada à realidade do ocultista e relevante ao seu contexto espiritual. Essa centelha Asetiana, uma marca subtil esculpida na alma, irá crescer e viver com o iniciado para toda a eternidade como um guia silencioso de luz violeta e uma bússola secreta dos mistérios; um aviso perpétuo de que os Asetianos ainda estão aqui e que a sua magia perdura nos pormenores mais simples da natureza.

Uma Palavra sobre Iniciação

A habilidade de ver, interpretar e compreender os mistérios que permanecem escondidos à vista de todos, é o que designamos por *iniciação*.

O conceito de iniciação é um dos mais incompreendidos no estudo do oculto, por vezes explorado e mal representado por aqueles que não entendem a verdadeira essência da magia iniciática. Em termos simples, alguém iniciado - em todas as sociedades ocultistas e escolas dos mistérios merecedoras do seu nome - é um indivíduo que tem a capacidade de ver o que outros não conseguem. O conceito não implica necessariamente que através de iniciação o ocultista tenha de desenvolver algum tipo de poder sobrenatural que o torne em algo superior à população mundana. Simplesmente significa que foi dada ao iniciado a chave secreta - o mistério - que lhe vai abrir as portas do conhecimento para que possa ver o que está escondido à vista do mundo. Aparentemente um conceito simples mas também altamente sofisticado. Pode ser visto como o caminho dos mistérios para alcançar a plenitude e superioridade, mas esse poder provém da sabedoria,

☥

compreensão e da verdade subtil encontrada apenas no interior de cada um e nunca através de qualquer mero exercício de poder místico.

Recorrendo a um simples exemplo, se visitar uma velha capela Cristã algures na Europa com um amigo que nunca tenha estudado ocultismo e observar um pentagrama esculpido numa das paredes de pedra - e isso não seria tão raro quanto se possa pensar - pode imediatamente fazer a ligação de que em algum momento na história a igreja e os seus fundadores tiveram, possivelmente, uma ligação secreta com feitiçaria tradicional Europeia ou algum envolvimento com alquimia e práticas pagãs. Dependendo do simbolismo presente e detalhes históricos envolventes, pode até ser possível definir que tradição específica seguiam e que tipo de práticas, rituais e crenças teriam. O amigo presente - aqui representando o não iniciado - provavelmente passaria pelo símbolo sem sequer reparar nele, pois a sua mente não está programada ou sintonizada para prestar atenção a simbolismo desconhecido, ignorando automaticamente muito do que é estranho ao seu código simbólico consciente. Mesmo que ele tivesse reparado no pentagrama iria muito provavelmente ignorá-lo.

Neste caso o leitor seria o iniciado, detendo a chave para um nível de compreensão e conhecimento que o seu amigo não teria. Saberia o *mistério* da iniciação em causa e, dessa forma, seria capaz de ver o que está escondido à vista de todos, enquanto que o mesmo permaneceria *invisível* para os outros. Esta é a verdadeira natureza da iniciação que a maioria das sociedades ocultistas mantiveram secreta durante tantos séculos.

Depois de ter revelado este conceito vital mas frequentemente incompreendido aos leitores deste *Liber*, irei explicar algumas chaves muito importantes no estudo dos mistérios do *Sigillum 333*.

Enquanto selo ritualístico e meditativo ele incorpora delicadamente o segredo de Orion através da linguagem secreta dos símbolos, da Kabbalah, do alfabeto Hebraico, da geometria sagrada e, claro, da tradição Asetiana. Estes pormenores, quando revelados ao estudante do oculto e adequadamente explorados em práticas metafísicas pessoais, irão equipar o iniciado com o conhecimento necessário para compreender, interpretar e explorar o sigilo de Orion, de forma a que nunca mais olhe para ele cegamente, tendo agora a capacidade para ver nele - e através dele - aquilo que outros não conseguem, tornando-se iniciado nos seus mistérios.

A iniciação desenvolve no ocultista as ferramentas que lhe permitem trabalhar - e pensar - a um outro nível de consciência, com uma compreensão mais profunda do que a da mente mundana. Uma vez iniciado nos mistérios, o estudante experiencia mudanças permanentes no seu mundo, sendo agora capaz de ver o que os outros não conseguem, com uma nova percepção da realidade assente no poder do conhecimento.

Muitos podem não gostar da confiança de um ocultista iniciado, podendo criticar, julgar ou condenar, sendo na realidade um reflexo de ausência de visão, não tendo o conhecimento para Ver através de olhos iniciados. Não é sensato discutir ou forçar entendimento numa mente que não foi iniciada, pois os seus pensamentos não irão fluir nem os seus olhos abrir para o mundo, simplesmente porque não conhecem a chave para ver o que o ocultista consegue. É o caminho correcto para o ocultista iniciado - e eu atrevo-me a dizer a única atitude evoluída e digna -, ignorar aqueles que o condenam de uma forma inferior e optar antes por meditar na renovada chama dos seus Olhos agora iniciados. Como eu sempre aconselho... usem-nos sabiamente.

O oculto sempre foi e continuará a ser um mundo rodeado de ilusão e armadilhas. Essa realidade deve ser vista como algo positivo visto ser o terreno ideal para métodos de iniciação, na medida em que, dessa forma, torna-se possível distinguir os fracos dos corajosos e os ignorantes dos sábios.

Se o ocultista não desenvolver um forte senso de consciência e percepção desde o início da sua viagem interior, irá eventualmente ficar preso numa das muitas armadilhas presentes no sinuoso caminho da sabedoria. É vital não desistir na primeira queda quando o iniciado tenta subir pela escada do conhecimento, mas sim lembrar-se que a verdadeira força do guerreiro é medida pela capacidade de se levantar novamente e admitir que falhou. De outra forma um passo em falso não lhe mostrará o segredo por detrás do véu do abismo abominável, mas poderá antes afogá-lo no oceano do esquecimento eterno. Esse fracasso encontra-se nos que, quando confusos pela aparente incapacidade de conquistar a sua própria espiritualidade e relevância no Universo, podendo finalmente observar a realidade escondida por detrás do véu dos velhos mistérios, tentam antes subir os degraus secretos da escada da iluminação através de mentiras e pela propagação da ilusão de uma falsa importância, em vez de simplesmente lutarem na escola da vida com honestidade e nobreza.

No amanhecer dos tempos continuamos confiantes no
nosso papel cósmico de iniciadores silenciosos.

Os Três Segredos

Três é um número mágico. Apesar de apenas um simples elemento matemático para os não iniciados, esconde na sua essência não só magia mas também conhecimento, pronto a ser descoberto, estudado e libertado pelo estudante do oculto.

No contexto deste *Liber*, Orion é examinada como uma expressão espiritual da fórmula mística do Três sagrado, onde as

✝

estrelas centrais que formam o cinturão da constelação - Alnitak, Alnilam e Mintaka - aparecem no centro destes ensinamentos. Elas incorporam uma poderosa expressão arquetípica de cada Linhagem Asetiana - Serpente, Escaravelho e Escorpião - assim como a fundação em símbolo para o caminho triplo de Morte, Vida e Renascimento, tão importante em qualquer tradição mística.

Esta relação com Orion e a sua cultura espiritual está presente ao longo de toda a história sob diversas formas de arquitectura ocultista. Os iniciados do Antigo Egipto, sendo notavelmente pioneiros, representaram a importância de Orion nas suas edificações religiosas, particularmente visível na tecnologia avançada - em termos de ciência, engenharia e metafísica - encontrada nos mais famosos templos iniciáticos da história, conhecidos como as Pirâmides, localizadas na necrópole de Gizé. As Pirâmides de Khufu, Khafre e Menkaure são um espelho simbólico do céu, funcionando como uma porta metafísica para o cosmos, edificadas por entre pó e o calor do deserto Egípcio. Quando alinhadas conceptualmente com Orion, as Pirâmides são uma expressão perfeita da formação das Linhagens Asetianas, tal como representadas na Árvore da Vida da Kabbalah. As três estrelas que se erguem no céu podem ser interpretadas como uma emanação espiritual dos três Primordiais acima do Abismo - no reino intemporal do Duat - enquanto que as Pirâmides presentes no plano físico expressam a sua manifestação terrena abaixo de Da'ath, como reflexo das três Linhagens incarnadas reflectindo os seus arquétipos superiores.

Uma compreensão mais profunda desta relação permite ver um significado ainda maior no legado de Thoth, sucintamente descrito através da fórmula *"As Above, so Below"* definindo uma importante base conceptual para a arquitectura da espiritualidade Asetiana. Numa tradução em Latim do trabalho lendário de Thoth, conhecido como a

Tábua de Esmeralda ou *Tabula Smaragdina*, também incluído na dissertação medieval *Secretum Secretorum*, originalmente em Árabe, encontramos a seguinte passagem:

> *"Quod est inferius est sicut quod est superius, et quod est superius est sicut quod est inferius, ad perpetranda miracula rei unius."*

A frase traduz-se para *"Aquilo que está abaixo é como aquilo que está acima e aquilo que está acima é como aquilo que está abaixo, para realizar os milagres do mistério uno."* Esta lei de Thoth está representada de uma forma muito concreta na terra sagrada do Egipto, onde as três Pirâmides reflectem a realidade superior das estrelas ao representarem Orion e os seus três mistérios interiores, tal como o microcosmo de cada indivíduo é também um reflexo do macrocosmo subtil escondido acima do Abismo. O Eu mundano é uma manifestação do Eu superior e este, por sua vez, é uma expressão do Eu Divino.

Para os leitores com especial atenção ao pormenor, poderão reparar que ao longo de todo o livro utilizei recorrentemente as palavras Morte, Vida e Renascimento nesta ordem em particular, enquanto que o resto do mundo refere este ciclo por uma ordem diferente: Vida, Morte e Renascimento. Esta mudança na ordem literária reflecte um paradigma importante da espiritualidade Asetiana, que está intimamente ligado à filosofia por detrás deste trabalho. Para uma mentalidade comum, a Vida no plano físico é o foco da sua realidade espiritual, reflectindo a ordem tradicional de Vida, Morte e Renascimento. As pessoas vêem a Vida como o objectivo principal e o centro da sua existência, por isso, naturalmente surge a Morte e depois o Renascimento através da reencarnação, regressando novamente à Vida e completando o ciclo. É desta forma que a grande maioria das religiões que adoptaram a reincarnação nas suas filosofias, expressam o ciclo perpétuo da sua realidade espiritual. Mas não o povo do Antigo Egipto...

No Asetianismo, a liberação absoluta não se manifesta através de um permanente regresso à Vida, mas sim por um retorno perpétuo à Morte. O Duat - império Egípcio dos mortos e submundo - é o verdadeiro reino da *vida* para uma mente Asetiana evoluída: o seu domínio nativo. A Vida é um estado impermanente e transitório, enquanto que a Morte é eterna, infinita e o berço da imortalidade. A Vida é uma escola poderosa de evolução espiritual, contudo meramente uma estrada no caminho universal que é o crescimento, enquanto que a Morte é o verdadeiro lar da alma: o trono do Eu Divino. A partir desta perspectiva espiritual, a Morte é na realidade muito mais genuína do que a Vida física, que em termos místicos representa uma ilusão poderosa e enganadora. Apesar desta visão poder parecer negra e mórbida à primeira vista, na realidade é uma perspectiva imensamente positiva e iluminada do percurso espiritual da alma. Tal como na mente avançada dos Antigos Egípcios, o foco está então na Morte e nos seus mistérios secretos; na quebra do condicionalismo da matéria e corpo, para uma dedicação à verdade encontrada no interior de cada um, sendo esta a única realidade que pode sobreviver à morte física. Isto não leva a uma visão triste e depressiva do mundo em que vivemos, mas sim a uma mentalidade iluminada que aprendeu a apreciar a vida no seu todo ao compreender a sua beleza impermanente e a valorizar cada momento. Com este segredo em mente, utilizei a fórmula de Morte, Vida e Renascimento como um detalhe literário iniciático escondido ao longo deste livro, pois os Asetianos encaram o ciclo espiritual tendo a Morte como o seu reino, a Vida como um percurso impermanente de aprendizagem e o Renascimento como o despertar para a Morte e a comunhão divina com Aset.

✝

"Vive como se fosses morrer amanhã. Aprende como se fosses viver para sempre."

Mahatma Gandhi

Os significados e conhecimento presentes nas fórmulas do Três sagrado são imensos e variados, não estando restritos aos paralelismos traçados neste texto. Eles estão representados na energia e simbolismo do *Sigillum 333* que, sendo um poderoso e complexo instrumento mágico, detém as chaves e os mistérios capazes de iniciar o estudante do oculto em níveis de conhecimento mais profundo enquanto se dedica ao estudo e trabalho esotérico com este sigilo. Numa breve referência ao *Book of Giza*, o primeiro trabalho incluído neste grimório triplo, torna-se relevante salientar que esse documento esotérico é formado por três Sebayt distintos, contendo cada um precisamente trinta e três revelações. Nada é ao acaso.

Para além da abundância de possíveis significados, nas páginas seguintes irei abordar e descrever três diferentes níveis de iniciação, derivados das fórmulas do Três sagrado e intimamente relacionados com o *Sigillum 333*, guiando o iniciado através de um poderoso trabalho espiritual de vital importância durante o estudo dos mistérios de Orion. Sendo um instrumento esotérico imbuído de energia e significado, o *Sigillum 333* apenas será útil e mostrará os seus segredos mais profundos aqueles que o utilizem com honestidade.

Sarcófago do Mundano

A Primeira Iniciação

A queda do Espírito para matéria é um processo espiritual descrito no Asetianismo como *From Purity to Dust*. A alma, enquanto encarnada, encontra-se fechada num sarcófago conceptual - o plano físico.

†

Compreender este processo e as suas implicações é de importância vital nas práticas e estudos iniciáticos através dos mistérios de Orion e da sua profunda mensagem de liberação. A filosofia inerente a este processo pode ser adequadamente compreendida durante o estudo do *Liber* יסוד, que inclui um capítulo dedicado ao desenvolvimento deste conceito e à sua relação metafísica com a Árvore da Vida.

Um mito clássico da antiga tradição Egípcia e que sobreviveu ao teste do tempo, é a história simbólica onde Seth engana e ilude Osiris, prendendo-o no interior de uma poderosa arca de ouro maciço, com o intuito de o privar dos seus poderes e da sua vida abençoada. Esta arca dourada representa o mundo material: é uma metáfora espiritual para a vida restrita e limitada do plano material.[18] Simboliza o desejo de Seth em manter a família real aprisionada num mundo supérfluo sem significado, em vez de livre para percorrer confiantemente o mundo que é seu domínio por direito - o reino de Energia e Espírito - e que Seth, na sua infinita ganância e inveja, queria para si próprio, levando-o ao seu maior objecto de desejo: o trono do Egipto. Presas neste estado de inconsciência e ilusão, trancadas dentro de uma prisão de aparências feita do ouro mais reluzente, a mente e a alma encontram-se ignorantes da sua existência absoluta e completa, bem como do seu verdadeiro potencial existente apenas fora daquela arca. A verdadeira identidade está adormecida e esquecida, vagueando como um sonho perdido, onde toda a realidade aparenta estar restrita a essas belas mas traiçoeiras paredes de ouro. Este é o mundo onde a humanidade se encontra aprisionada e adormecida; a realidade cega e ignorante do plano material, a verdadeira expressão de futilidade e ego. Para a maioria das pessoas, estas paredes conceptuais de corpo e matéria, erguidas pelas leis do plano físico, representam a sua visão completa da realidade, vivendo num sonho fútil acreditando que isso é tudo o que realmente importa. Inconsciente do enorme, invisível e subtil mundo, repleto de possibilidades, que existe para lá da jaula do corpo e da matéria, quem não é realmente livre e iniciado não consegue ver para lá das suas próprias limitações e compreender como tudo o que acredita ser valioso e importante, é na realidade supérfluo e insignificante no grande esquema do Universo.

Este é um dos mais básicos segredos do domínio e influência Sethiana, assim como um reflexo da perigosa realidade que se esconde por detrás do seu poder; uma expressão mítica de um legado de controlo e ignorância, manifestado em absoluto no plano onde detêm o seu maior poder - o domínio físico e reino de matéria onde as almas adormecidas estão aprisionadas. Esta influência Sethiana está reflectida na última era espiritual - o *Djehuty do Crocodilo* - que é historicamente marcada pelo aparecimento e proliferação da escravidão religiosa através do dogma e pelo medo da divindade e poder divino, assim como por uma crescente valorização da posse material e a sua decadência espiritual. Entretanto, as realidades subtis que edificaram a supremacia dos velhos impérios, como a magia, os mistérios e a natureza, sofreram as consequências do arrogante e ignorante pensamento moderno, sendo menosprezadas e rejeitadas pela humanidade, os seres providos do mais poderoso intelecto entre todos os animais e, portanto, espiritualmente responsáveis por proteger o seu verdadeiro tesouro natural.[19]

Sem esta iniciação para um estado de maior consciência e conhecimento, a alma leva uma vida cega, sem um vislumbre da bela, poderosa e libertadora realidade que se esconde mesmo por cima das suas cabeças e à sua volta, mas que não pode dessa forma ver, sentir ou tocar, levando a uma convicção generalizada de que essa realidade simplesmente não existe. Essa ausência de visão espiritual - o aprisionamento da alma em matéria - não é apenas manifestada por aqueles que não aceitam o seu lado espiritual, mas também, muitas

†

vezes de modo ainda mais destruidor, por aqueles que se consideram espirituais e evoluídos quando, na realidade, continuam presos nos túneis mais profundos do seu túmulo físico, abraçando uma vida de escravidão absoluta totalmente controlada pelos ideais de riqueza, juventude, posse, reconhecimento e aparência. Simplesmente porque alguém tenta estudar o oculto, professa uma vida espiritual ou acredita possuir uma mente mística capaz de pensamentos profundos, isso por si só não implica qualquer nível de iluminação, conhecimento ou consciência. Na verdade, muitas das representações vãs e supérfluas de personalidade que são encontradas em mentes que estudam o oculto são, frequentemente, uma triste expressão do ego, insegurança e ilusão.

Esta mentalidade e filosofia são importantes no estudo do oculto e merecedoras de longa meditação e aprendizagem, bem como representativas de uma grande conquista para qualquer iniciado da tradição Asetiana. Este conhecimento e iniciação são uma marca que distingue um Asetiano ou um verdadeiro Asetianista de uma mente inferior, sendo assim livre e completo da forma mais profunda e libertadora. Através desta cultura e caminho espiritual, o iniciado experiencia em primeira mão a forma mais pura e poderosa de liberdade, ao quebrar e abrir o seu próprio sarcófago - a iniciação para o conhecimento e compreensão - tornando-se livre para explorar o reino espiritual e dominar as energias em completa consciência de todo o seu potencial.

Assim que a prisão de matéria é quebrada, esta não poderá ser selada novamente. Quando o iniciado alcança um estado mental de tal liberdade espiritual - encontrando assim um breve vislumbre do Universo como observado pelos Olhos de um Asetiano - ele não poderá ser cegado novamente e a sua consciência é então libertada para abraçar todo o alcance do espectro do seu próprio potencial. Este processo alquímico de evolução espiritual manifesta o conceito filosófico e metafórico de que a maior parte das pessoas que são capazes de ver a *cores* estão apenas a experienciar uma poderosa ilusão. Na realidade, apenas conseguem ver verdadeiramente em tons de cinzento, vivendo na ilusão de que o que vêem é o espectro total das cores e dessa forma assumindo ser essa a manifestação total do arco-íris. Mas a partir do momento em que se alcança um primeiro vislumbre de cor verdadeira, sendo assim capaz de se olhar pelos Olhos de um Asetiano, mesmo que apenas por um milésimo de segundo, então todo um novo Universo aparece em frente dos olhos agora iniciados. Esta é a verdadeira iniciação... e ela é eterna.

> *"Assim que aprendidas as ferramentas que permitem ver através de uma perspectiva Asetiana, a alma é transformada para sempre, sendo incapaz de se tornar cega novamente."*
>
> Tânia Fonseca

A primeira iniciação de Orion está representada de uma forma bastante marcada no Arcano Maior XVI do Tarot - A Torre. Sendo uma expressão cataclísmica de destruição suprema, esta carta, tal como muitas outras, é frequentemente mal interpretada. O colapso da inabalável estrutura que é a torre simboliza a ruptura com crenças ultrapassadas através da libertação da sua prisão no plano material. O processo pode ser doloroso e por vezes até devastador, mas tem a capacidade de libertar o iniciado dos condicionalismos do mundano e da estagnação e limites impostos pela sociedade. Deve liberar a alma e abrir os caminhos. Os iniciados que tenham destruído os alicerces subtis da sua torre interior e sobrevivido, conquistaram dessa forma a liberdade mais pura, absoluta e incondicional. Apenas nos tempos mais devastadores surgem as formas mais profundas de liberação.

✝

O conceito do *despertar* - o *awakening* -, frequentemente estudado no Asetianismo e tão intimamente relacionado com a tradição vampírica, detém uma forte correlação espiritual com o mistério que descrevi em o *Sarcófago do Mundano*. A destruição do sarcófago do plano físico e a conquista da independência de todas as formas de condicionalismo mundano, através da sabedoria espiritual, é uma forma poderosa de magia e conquista pessoal que traz o domínio sob a existência subtil e oculta - mas claramente mais real - de volta para as mãos do iniciado. Este processo esotérico representa uma manifestação complexa do conceito metafísico de *awakening*, profundamente escondido e enraizado enquanto marca essencial da espiritualidade vampírica, tão incompreendida pelos não iniciados ainda fechados dentro da sua própria prisão mística.

Deve ainda ser explicado que a compreensão desta importante forma de iniciação não significa que qualquer aspecto mundano deva ser ignorado e rejeitado, ou que a vida no plano material é obrigatoriamente uma forma de existência insignificante e obsoleta. Pelo contrário, a vida enquanto incarnada neste mundo é uma oportunidade única de aprender e evoluir de variadas formas que uma mera existência subtil não potenciaria. Cabe ao indivíduo fazer uma escolha consciente e tomar as decisões mais adequadas, de forma a abraçar a vida em todo o seu potencial para a aprendizagem espiritual, ou simplesmente desperdiçá-la em ilusões supérfluas. Na realidade, o poder mais puro e verdadeiro vive dentro de cada um. O mundo material permite a compreensão e liberação da verdadeira Vontade, bem como manifestar a chama da iluminação, depois de purificada nos planos superiores da existência subtil. No entanto, para conquistar esse estado de liberdade absoluta, de forma a dominar o plano físico e manifestar a essência interior, é necessário primeiro lutar e destruir as armadilhas traiçoeiras da matéria.

†

Este é um dos mistérios aprofundados pelos ocultistas envolvidos com a alquimia da alma e a razão pela qual os alquimistas da antiguidade e os mestres da Kabbalah abordam o elemento Terra como um elemental inferior. Enquanto examinei e descrevi a língua Hebraica no *Liber* יסוד, tive o cuidado de explicar que as três letras primárias do alfabeto místico são Aleph א, Mem מ e Shin ש, representando os três elementos maiores da alquimia - Ar, Água e Fogo. O elemento Terra é intencionalmente não representado no alfabeto Hebraico pois na Kabbalah esta força universal é vista como menor e espiritualmente menos poderosa do que outras três. A razão metafísica e filosófica inerente a esta aparente omissão reside precisamente no mistério que defini como o *Sarcófago do Mundano*. Terra permanece um poderoso elemental, sendo contudo um elemento ilusório e limitador que o ocultista tem de aprender a quebrar e dominar, de forma a obter controlo e poder sob os outros três; sendo eles os que verdadeiramente manifestam o mundo espiritual.

Agora está revelado o segredo alquímico escondido no pensamento místico da queda do Espírito para matéria - *From Purity to Dust*. Estes ensinamentos manifestam a realização e compreensão por parte do iniciado, da condição da alma após o momento de reencarnação - a sua prisão no sarcófago do mundano. Este é o mistério espiritual principal, estudado e ensinado profundamente no interior da maioria das sociedades secretas ao longo da história, presentes desde os tempos mais remotos até à era actual. É esta também a primeira iniciação de Orion; a quebra e conquista do túmulo decadente onde a Ba permanece escondida e afastada do seu potencial absoluto. Mas, enquanto primeira iniciação, este é apenas o primeiro passo até Orion...

✝

Mistérios Revelados

A Segunda Iniciação

Neste capítulo o leitor irá iniciar o trabalho esotérico referente ao estudo e análise dos diferentes elementos presentes na simbologia do *Sigillum 333*. Se nunca utilizou o selo de Orion em práticas metafísicas, ou se não está familiarizado com o trabalho mágico específico através deste sigilo e cujas chaves se encontram escondidas no estudo do seu simbolismo, é então sugerido que seja dedicado algum tempo ao uso independente do sigilo e à sua exploração em meditação e ritual antes de examinar este capítulo. Em magia cerimonial, o sigilo pode ser reproduzido por um método à escolha do ocultista e da sua preferência, sendo frequentemente ilustrado à mão num processo mágico de criação artística, não limitado pela pressão e imposição temporal. Este objecto mágico criado pelo ocultista será depois destruído numa prática ritual complexa, onde será consumido pelo calor da chama, tendo os quatro elementais como testemunhas, quebrando assim as energias artísticas usadas na sua criação e manifestando a mensagem secreta da sua essência no interior da mente do iniciado.

A complexidade deste sigilo e a simbologia nele incluída é imensa, pelo que a exploração de todos os aspectos e correlações presentes nos seus diferentes elementos seria material suficiente para elaborar um livro inteiro. Contudo, durante as próximas páginas irei guiar o leitor num estudo estruturado pelos elementos iniciáticos principais do sigilo e da sua formação, explorando o simbolismo fundamental do selo e revelando o significado mágico associado a cada nível de sabedoria presente. Ao longo desta análise será importante usar como referência contínua o sigilo incluído na capa do *Liber*.

Começando pelo centro do selo mágico, podemos observar a representação das sete estrelas principais da constelação astronómica de Orion, que formam o que anteriormente designamos como o sigilo

✝

natural de Orion ou sigilo interno, aqui ilustrado no interior de um círculo preto que simboliza o céu - e todo o Universo - através da forma circular, um velho símbolo do conceito de perfeição e a personificação geométrica do absoluto.

Exteriormente ao círculo preto universal encontra-se um hexagrama com seis símbolos, divididos em dois grupos distintos de coloração invertida - os hieróglifos Egípcios referentes ás três Linhagens Asetianas a preto com fundo branco e três letras do alfabeto Grego desenhadas a branco num fundo preto.

Os símbolos Egípcios para as Linhagens bem como o seu significado elementar não requerem qualquer introdução para um estudante da magia Asetiana, contudo as letras Gregas podem parecer uma surpresa para alguns. Elas são utilizadas neste sigilo devido à sua importância científica e histórica em termos de astronomia, pois relacionam-se com as três estrelas do cinturão de Orion - ζ é a letra Zeta e simboliza Alnitak, ε é a letra Epsilon e representa Alnilam e δ é a letra Delta e expressa Mintaka.

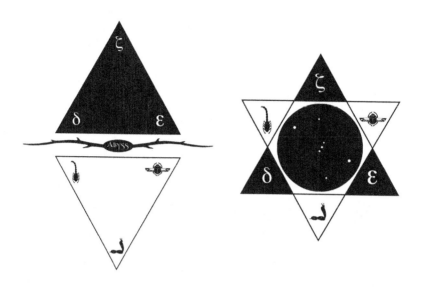

O que pode não ser perceptível à superfície é que este hexagrama é na realidade a união de dois triângulos opostos. O primeiro em preto com a representação das estrelas - a realidade divina - e o segundo em branco com a representação das Linhagens - a manifestação terrena das estrelas superiores abaixo do Abismo.

Quando cruzados e unidos pela transcendência do Abismo alquímico, permitem a refracção de luz espiritual e tornam visível a verdade universal no seu núcleo, cujo segredo é aqui representado pelo sigilo natural de Orion. Tal como duas lentes mágicas e poderosas que, quando colocadas uma por cima da outra pelas mãos dos Anciãos, podem revelar uma imagem escondida dos mistérios - o verdadeiro segredo.

Como se pode agora compreender, estes dois triângulos revelam o mistério da queda do Espírito para matéria - *From Purity to Dust* - através do processo de formação da Árvore da Vida, conforme descrito no *Liber* יסוד. Quando os triângulos - representações simbólicas e bidimensionais de uma pirâmide, aqui ilustrados em posições opostas -

são deslocados de forma a se unirem, formam uma entidade única, definindo a figura geométrica conhecida como hexagrama. Quando o hexagrama está formado, os arquétipos das Linhagens e as suas emanações divinas estão agora alinhados em triângulos menores opostos - Alnitak e Khufu estão alinhados com a Serpente; Alnilam e Khafre opõem-se ao Escaravelho e, por último, Mintaka e Menkaure alinham-se com o símbolo do Escorpião. Estudantes da Kabbalah experientes podem ver os domínios mais transcendentes da Árvore da Vida - o mundo de Atziluth a preto e o de Briah a branco - devidamente representados no sigilo, tal como as duas tríades superiores de sephiroth, que aparecem nas posições correctas em cada triângulo deste segredo: Kether, Chokmah e Binah a preto; Chesed, Geburah e Tiphareth a branco. O simbolismo do sigilo ilustra a tríade de emanações divinas - aqui representadas por Alnitak, Alnilam e Mintaka - e as suas incarnações terrenas, manifestadas abaixo de Da'ath, representadas pelos hieróglifos das três Linhagens.

O hexagrama, sendo a união de dois triângulos opostos, um normal e outro invertido, esconde uma mensagem simbólica adicional de grande valor metafísico. Os dois triângulos são também os símbolos alquímicos tradicionais para Fogo e Água; as duas grandes forças antagónicas do Universo. Ao combiná-las no interior da mente e da alma, através da magia deste sigilo, é possível alcançar a alquimia suprema edificada pela perfeita união de opostos - o Hexagrama: uma poderosa representação de estabilidade e equilíbrio espiritual.

Este é o grande segredo do simbolismo do hexagrama, tal como estudado no interior da Aset Ka e um conhecimento iniciático que o leitor pode agora compreender enquanto ele permanece escondido à vista de todos, pois agora um simples hexagrama nunca mais irá parecer o mesmo. A sua mensagem espiritual é profunda e transformacional, mas assim que devidamente compreendida e assimilada torna-se clara e bela na sua simplicidade. Este significado secreto está também representado inequivocamente no Arcano Maior XIV do Tarot - Temperança - que na ilustração tradicional mostra uma figura alada com um triângulo gravado no peito a praticar as artes mágicas, misturando um fluido místico desconhecido entre dois cálices dourados. Esta é a carta infame que o ocultista Aleister Crowley modificou o nome na sua versão pessoal do Tarot, chamando-lhe Arte, e gerando muita controvérsia entre os não iniciados. Esta *Arte* à qual Crowley se refere é nada mais nada menos do que a unificação das forças opostas presentes na dualidade, sendo a alquimia interna do ocultista. Na sua versão do Tarot, Frieda Harris ilustrou uma figura com duas cabeças, vertendo Água e Fogo para um caldeirão mágico.

Esse simbolismo ilustra de uma forma literal a união mística entre Fogo e Água, os dois elementos alquímicos representados pelos triângulos opostos que formam o nosso hexagrama. A figura de duas cabeças, que mistura os elementos através da suas artes mágicas, representa a união perfeita entre o Rei e a Rainha, mas Crowley e Harris foram ainda mais longe no simbolismo que incluíram nesta carta, pois esta entidade andrógina é desenhada controversamente com seis seios que, como agora se pode compreender, representam os seis triângulos menores presentes no nosso hexagrama.

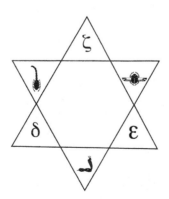

À medida que aprofundamos o estudo dos mistérios presentes na alquimia espiritual do *Sigillum 333*, depois de compreender o pormenor iniciático e revelador de que o hexagrama representa, quando observado pela mente mística, a união de dois importantes símbolos alquímicos, o leitor pode então observar a presença de dois triângulos menores no topo do hexagrama e outros dois abaixo, no interior do sigilo. Estes são os reconhecidos símbolos alquímicos utilizados nas artes mágicas para representar as quatro forças elementais do Universo - Fogo, Água, Ar e Terra.

Na mitologia do Antigo Egipto, estes poderosos elementos estavam associados ao conceito teológico dos *Quatro Filhos de Horus*, conhecidos por Imset, Qebehsenuf, Duamutef e Hapi - os quatro vasos canópicos utilizados no processo de mumificação e na magia desses velhos rituais de imortalidade.[20][21]

O método tradicional de pensamento e prática mágica é na realidade um exercício de fórmulas profundamente científicas. Os poderes dos verdadeiros alquimistas e ocultistas iniciados, descritos como os quatro elementais, estão correctamente representados nas ciências modernas, extensivamente estudados na física e na química como os quatro estados da matéria: sólido, líquido, gasoso e plasma.

As propriedades físicas do estado sólido tem correspondência com as qualidades do elemento Terra, tal como os líquidos são comparáveis à Água alquímica, gases relacionam-se com Ar e plasma, naturalmente, é relacionável com o Fogo mágico.

Estes elementos presentes no sigilo interligam dois arquétipos de Linhagens distintas, deixando pistas a possíveis implicações alquímicas entre emanações duplas de diferentes Linhagens. Cada elemento aparece representado entre uma emanação superior e outra inferior, mas nunca da mesma Linhagem. Por exemplo, o símbolo do Fogo está entre o ζ de Alnitak, associado à Serpente divina, e o

✝

hieróglifo do Escorpião incarnado, enquanto que o símbolo para a Terra está localizado entre o ε de Alnilam, ligado ao Escaravelho divino, e o hieróglifo da Serpente incarnada.

Estas correlações esboçam uma filosofia de extrema complexidade e as suas práticas metafísicas, difíceis de compreender numa primeira abordagem, estando relacionadas com o potencial de interacção energética entre a essência de duas Linhagens diferentes. Esse conhecimento pode ser explorado e aprofundado na alquimia da alma através de práticas mágicas avançadas, enquanto define um sistema ritualístico elaborado relativamente aos processos de evocação em magia cerimonial Asetiana.

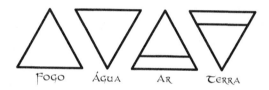

FOGO   ÁGUA   AR   TERRA

De cada lado do hexagrama ilustrado no nosso sigilo encontram-se dois hieróglifos do Ankh ☥ - um em posição normal e outro invertido.

Este hieróglifo intemporal era de importância vital na velha tradição do Antigo Egipto, sendo considerado sagrado e frequentemente representado nas mãos dos Deuses. Em termos de linguagem, o seu significado é traduzido de uma forma literal para *Vida* e está relacionado com a filosofia Asetiana de imortalidade. Sozinho é um sigilo de poder inquestionável, assumindo um dos maiores legados simbólicos da história, com uma vasta implicação mágica e espiritual, e que apesar de frequentemente mal representado e interpretado nos tempos modernos, todo o alcance da sua magia e poder estão fora do propósito deste *Liber*.

☥

Os dois Ankh incluídos neste sigilo escondem vários significados a nível oculto, mas o que iremos revelar neste estudo está relacionado com *Os Pilares dos Mistérios*. Conforme explicado no *Liber* יסוד, o lado esquerdo da Árvore da Vida, manifestado pelas sephiroth Binah, Geburah e Hod - diferentes emanações do arquétipo de Escorpião - é conhecido como o Pilar de Esquerda e manifesta a representação espiritual do nosso lado sombrio, aqui ilustrado por um Ankh invertido à esquerda do sigilo. Ao observar a Árvore da Vida representada no sigilo, é possível verificar-se que, estando posicionado entre o Escorpião e δ, este Ankh invertido aparece correctamente localizado e com precisão entre Geburah e Binah.

Do lado direito da Árvore encontramos Chokmah, Chesed e Netzach como emanações do Escaravelho, aqui ilustrados pelo Ankh em posição normal; a nossa face de luz. Posicionado no sigilo entre o Escaravelho e ε, o Ankh aparece ao lado de Chesed e Chokmah quando visualizamos a Árvore da Vida e as suas sephiroth. Com este conhecimento, a representação de Orion através das suas sete estrelas no centro do sigilo pode também ser interpretada como um Ankh secreto, simbolizando o Pilar de Equilíbrio - Middle Pillar -, personificando a união de forças opostas, devida e subtilmente localizada em símbolo entre ζ e a Serpente - Kether e Tiphareth - as duas primeiras sephiroth do Pilar de Equilíbrio na Árvore da Vida.

O estudo destas correlações e o seu simbolismo, conjugando conhecimento proveniente de várias tradições, culturas e formas de sabedoria, pode parecer confuso numa primeira abordagem. Mas é por essa razão que são recomendadas várias leituras deste documento durante o processo de estudo do sigilo, até que todos os elementos e a sua relevância estejam devidamente compreendidos e perfeitamente assimilados.

Ao chegar à margem exterior do sigilo neste estudo, encontra-se uma circunferência preta com seis letras do alfabeto Hebraico. Este alfabeto é de importância vital em diversos aspectos do conhecimento da Kabbalah, tendo sido também utilizado na origem do desenvolvimento do misticismo ocidental e aí estudado durante séculos.

A sua importância, simbolismo e desenvolvimento esotérico podem ser compreendidos durante o estudo do *Liber* יסוד, onde o leitor pode aprender o segredo por detrás da formação das vinte e duas letras que o compõem. Estas pequenas e curvilíneas letras-sigilo correspondem a cada um dos vinte e dois percursos iniciáticos que interligam as dez sephiroth da Árvore da Vida, assim como aos vinte e dois Arcanos Maiores do Tarot tradicional. Torna-se então claro como cada letra Hebraica personifica o simbolismo de cada um dos caminhos espirituais encontrados neste sistema, ilustrados de forma tão única e mística através de arte e cor nas pinturas presentes nas cartas de Tarot.

No sigilo de Orion - que descrevemos como *Sigillum 333* - as seis letras Hebraicas representadas no círculo externo, estão localizadas perto do vértice geométrico de cada um dos seis triângulos individuais, gerados pela união dos elementos alquímicos Fogo e Água, conforme estudado anteriormente. Adoptando uma progressão geométrica retrógrada, ou seja, no sentido horário, as letras Hebraicas são: Vav ו, Kaph כ, He ה, Beth ב, Gimel ג e Yod י. Duas letras para cada linhagem, numa manifestação divina e terrena das suas energias. Novamente... dualidade.

Entre Alnitak ζ e a Serpente encontramos as letras Vav ו e Beth ב. Vav ו representa o arquétipo do mestre iluminado, relacionado com o Arcano Maior V do Tarot - O Hierofante -, um símbolo universal da ligação inescrutável entre o humano e o divino; uma ponte entre o sagrado e o profano. Beth ב, enquanto uma expressão de conhecimento e sabedoria, está ligada ao Arcano Maior I do Tarot - O Mago - que, no seu infindável poder místico, esconde também o perigo da ausência de consciência.

Perto de Alnilam ε e do Escaravelho encontramos as letras He ה e Kaph כ. He ה é uma personificação de pureza e das energias transformacionais, estando relacionado com o Arcano Maior XVII do Tarot - A Estrela -, que deixa uma mensagem de esperança, possibilidade e eternidade. Kaph כ está ligado ao dinamismo e movimento, que através do Arcano Maior X do Tarot - Roda da Fortuna - deixa a chave para novos começos, dúvidas, instabilidade e destino.

Em Mintaka δ e no Escorpião encontramos os caracteres Gimel ג e Yod י. Gimel ג é uma letra de influência lunar profunda, associada ao Arcano Maior II do Tarot - A Sacerdotiza. Como iniciatriz, ela representa um arquétipo de intuição, confiança e força determinada mas delicada. Yod ' incorpora a escuridão e introspecção através do Arcano Maior IX do Tarot - O Eremita -, uma visão mística da pura rejeição do mundano e um símbolo da incessante busca pela luz interior, por vezes também relacionado com isolamento e solidão.

É importante compreender que todas estas cartas e o seu universo simbólico expressam arquétipos espirituais universais, que representam ideias e iniciações profundas, não emoções ou características psicológicas, e por isso não devem ser interpretadas de uma forma simplista ou superficial. As suas mensagens ocultas e significados reveladores são complexos e profundos, na medida em que cada carta representa um Arcano Maior do Tarot, que em Latim significa *Grande Segredo*, estando aqui representados apenas seis dos vinte e dois possíveis caminhos da vida do iniciado, a partir do momento em que inicia a sua conquista interior de evolução espiritual através dos mundos da Árvore da Vida. Uma vez mais chamo a atenção para o facto de que as cartas de Tarot serem aqui referidas, assim como os seus significados arquetípicos, não implica que representem uma tentativa de categorizar ou definir qualquer Linhagem Asetiana. São usadas neste contexto como expressões iniciáticas da dualidade presente nas emanações energéticas de cada Linhagem, particularmente devido ás suas posições acima e abaixo do Abismo de Da'ath, na Árvore da Vida. Associar de uma forma simples e independente os mistérios de um Arcano do Tarot com uma Linhagem específica, seria um erro.

Como último detalhe, estão presentes no sigilo três círculos de diferente diâmetro e espessura; uma última homenagem ao poder e simbolismo escondido em algo aparentemente tão simples... o número Três.

O mistério final e a chave suprema deste segredo levam-nos de volta ao início deste estudo e encontra-se na própria forma de Orion, conforme observável no céu nocturno, encantando o corpo iniciático de Nut. É por esta razão que essa ilustração mágica ocupa a posição central no sigilo, imbuído dos ensinamentos dos velhos mestres.

A beleza encontra-se nos detalhes e é apenas alcançada através da simplicidade.

Chave de Orion
A Terceira Iniciação

0. Ah o vazio do Louco! Através da Chave dos mistérios a iniciação manifesta-se escondida em Três.

1. Escondida na mais obscura face de Nut encontra-se a Chave para este mistério.

2. Nas horas de escuridão da luz interior consome o Seu corpo nú e conseguirás ver!

3. A fórmula que chega de Cima é três igual a um e um igual a um mais um de forma a que três iguale sete.

4. O Esplendor vive em Beleza mas a Beleza vive em Força.

5. Para Coroares o Eu não deves procurar Sabedoria mas acordar a Compreensão.

6. O Reino é para os fracos e cegos pois precisas de te libertar dessa prisão.

7. A sua Beleza pode ser sedutora mas apenas em três poderá o não coroado ver acima do Abismo.

8. Três originaram três e outros três e só então todos se tornaram um.

9. O véu temporal será agora fechado pois esta é a hora de o selar pelo interior.

☥

Liber Vox I

L *iber Vox I* is a small compilation of Asetian poetry and hymns that describe historical occurrences, spiritual views and lost voices of our shared past. A few of these poems were written several years ago during metaphysical rituals while others were driven from intensive past-life work through the Akashic records. As some passages express real historical events, emotions and voices, examined in detail within the Aset Ka, their spiritual and inspirational value is undeniable. They are not meant to be a perfectly harmonious expression of the Elder days, but instead a raw account with its due pain and darkness. Although brief and simple, they carry strong emotions and profound feelings that can easily be felt by those able to raise their awareness. They express fear, confusion and agonizing pain, but also hope, honor and loyalty. The content, message and reality expressed within the seven distinctive works included in this iteration of *Liber Vox* are personal and even intimate. Not all words are intended to be interpreted literally, as some echo metaphors and imply deeper meaning than words can convey. As the first volume of the *Liber Vox* series to be released openly in an international publication, this document represents a subtle sample of Asetian emotion carved in paper and ink.

These voices are footprints of a long forgotten past.
Explore them with an open heart...

The Call of Serket

Asetian Hymn of the Scorpion

Sia Deshret

Hepet Sedjet

Khenmet Aset

Hepet Senef

Kheper Mesha'

A'nen Nefer

Kem Hu Sekhem

✝

Knowledge of the Desert

Embrace the Flame

Kiss of Aset

Embrace the Blood

Become the Army

Bring back the Beauty

The Black World of Inner Power

✝

A Burning Empire

Where once stood color, life and prosperity

Now rules shadow and flame

The South has come to the North

The West moved towards the East

We can hear the cries of the Nile

As the wind blows on our faces

An Empire silent in shame

Forgotten deeds of old

Broken arrows and splinted swords

Blood has taken over

Pain is in your call

Anger is in your breath

Suffering is in your demand

Oh black land where are your Gods?

Why do you burn in silence?

Why do you cry in vain?

Help us... we are hopeless my Lord

Where are our rulers?

That brought us out of shadow into gold

Are they sleeping with our dying soldiers?

In a sleep of eternal silence

Reaching the depths of oblivion

People of the Flame please return to us

Hear our desperate call

Rise again, Powers of the Abyss

Claim once more what belongs to You

Oh Flame that burns in shades of Violet

Your Land is calling for You

May the Serpents Bite

May the Scorpions Sting

May the Scarabs Bind

Oh yes, I can hear You all from distance

In a silent whisper that will freeze the Desert

The Jackals have left the grounds of the dead

Now is the time

Now is the hour

The Red Flame will be touched by the hands of storm

The Lords of Kemet are returning

Let us all welcome their aid in glory

May you rise with one thousand arrows

And the Empire shall be forever Yours

Oh people of Kemet hear my call

TO WAR!!!

Framework

A hopeless burning Kemet from the war against the Sethian horde. A sea of lifeless bodies surrounded by pain, fear and confusion. Echo of the desperate thoughts from an elderly devout peasant, lost in the middle of the field of battle, in a small forgotten village of the Asetian Empire.

☥

Cries of a Loyal Scorpion

Loyal Scorpion of the Bloodline
In sadness you keep your eternal watch
Like a dead rose, dry from the centuries
Solitary Woman the world shall never comprehend
In silence you bring forth your magick
And in the mist you condemn the Sin
Perturbed is your fingerprint's feel
Slow are the tides of your inner thought
One of the condemned you have become
In a life of sorrow and darkness
Black is the color of your heart
Stained by the tint of immortal pain
Undecipherable is your ethereal gaze
In a code of madness and rage
Your energy shakes down the elements
In a dance of pride and shame
Decisive are all your silent moves
In a powerful tapestry of love and hate
For no one shall ever see your glimpse
A being of such forgotten beauty
The royal obelisk of poisonous protection
In your hope you hide away your fears

And your tides flow to the netherworld

Strong claws of ageless wars

Wipe out the tears that met the Nile

Pray in silence for the right momentum

For in the age of the darkest of days

Your subtle paws shall ever preside

No one hears your silent whispers

No one dares to break your code

Walking invisibly among the living

Dark angel of your beloved

Feared enemy of your opposers

True adversary of mortal kin

In your own solitary sarcophagus

You strike wisely for your cryptic gain

The Red Dawn

The Birth of Neith

A new dawn is rising

The red crown of Ra emerges in the East

Whispers of a nameless shadow

Unspoken words of trembling voices

Shaken grasps of dying hearts

Our night was one of painful sin

Blood has been spilled in the fields

Bodies found emerging from the filth in the river

The taste in our mouth is that of iron

Red is now the world as we see it

As the Sun rises high once more

The lament of the young widows

The pale faces of their newborn daughters

We have lived to watch our world collapse

Under our bare feet remain the empty stones

Edifications of once mighty temples

Strongholds of our precious Empire

☥

Our peace was shaken by fire and stone

The lives claimed by the fist with a sword

Taken by surprise and cunning treachery

Drowned in our pride our night has ended

Oh mighty island of our Lady

Who would dare to strike right unto our heart?

How deep goes the wound inflicted upon us

Shall our enemies never fight with honor?

But history unfolds in the most unexpected ways

And the Violet Flame acts in mysterious perfection

Maybe were the stars so perfectly aligned?

Or did the wild birds sing unanimously in chorus?

Oh Seth how deeply your arrogance betrayed you

An army wanting to sing your hymns of victory

No one steps uninvited into Asetian holy ground

And in the time when your horde was striking

Right between your malignant plans to kill and burn

An unforeseen star was born in the Elder sky

†

A child, that fought as a woman

A slave, that learned how to sting

Carved in the laws of the ancient desert

An untamed animal beneath golden skin

Among fire and red flame her love surfaced

Her weakened eyes shed tears in pain

A striking arrow pierced through the shadows

No mind was needed; no life, no gain

She put her love above the pain

And brought herself into the Flame

In an embrace of eternal claim

He gave her death, but took it away

In a soft and gentle Kiss

Their cursed lips betrayed life

And a mighty warrior was soon to rise

Years from this day her time will come

Blessed by the fierceness of her youth

You shall regret the daemon you awoken today

For she shall rise upon your cries

And inflict the strike of her divine bow

☥

Oh Seth what did you do?

So condemned you have now become

For Neith was born in this painful night

Oh for the love of Aset

Neith was born in this Red Dawn!

"I am the things that are, that will be, and that have been.

No mortal has yet been able to lift the veil that covers Me."

Temple of Neith. Sa el-Hagar, Egypt

Framework

The painful dawn following a sudden Sethian attack at the heart of the Asetian Empire in the sacred island of Philae. The ultimate sacrifice of a young girl and the birth of a legendary Scorpion warrior known as Neith.

☥

Child of Khufu

Behind a veil of memory and time
In curly hair she was then seen
Of darker color in shades of brown
A tender expression she carried with joy
In an immortal gaze she turned to see

Who this divine child might be?
To play in such unexpected place
In bare feet against sand and stone
Oh down the wider walkway she ran
In the grounds of Khufu, she remains

Peaceful guardian of the elder temple
How innocent is your untroubled smile
Is the rage hidden deep within you?
For a fierce lioness shall bloom one day
As the age of your gaze cannot hide the real you

Oh gentle creature of the sands
My honorable princess of eternal lands
May your feline paws guide our hearts into safety
And from all our foes keep the Empire at bail

✝

Our trust lies blindly in you

For loyalty is your strongest clue

Like no human can ever perceive

Your dedication feeds our needs and deeds

So life springs forth in the beauty of our path

In sepia eyes reflecting our desert

One of the Pyramids you once became

An initiatory temple your body prevails

Oh hidden priestess of silent mystery

Stronghold of our immortality

Lady of Khufu please look at us

We adore you, but we fear you

For your coldness chills us out in the night

And your heat brings us forth in the day

That was the sight of a timeless girl

A young child beneath forbidden stone

Among the most noble daughters of the ancient land

In the holy temples she walked as her home

For an immortal predator she ultimately became...

✝

The Prophecy

Art is achieved when the mind is not seeking
A formless pattern in the chaos of emotion
Sought by the lost and found by the humble
In a timeless dance of mysterious stumble

A secret is found only to be forgotten
In the chest of your thoughts locked within metal
Away from the truth but close to the heart
In the most vain of clues we can see your true chain

Empowered by desire and condemned by fear
You dream of a world that I painted in the night
Ghastly remembered in the time of tomorrow
Floating in the mourning shimmer of crimson light

Marriage of forces
Union of strength
Vindication of corpses
Justice in the land

The pain was achieved

In silence, uncovered

Through color and smoke

The name was engraved

Allegiance was sworn

Carved in water and stone

The beauty was shown

Right beneath the pillar alone

The destiny was reached

Through sorrow and tomb

A prophecy was fulfilled

His legacy renown

The Return

In the lost horizon a binding light peeked in silence
Old gestures remembered by the sleep of forgotten minds
The mist of confusion gave birth to clarity and determination
While the eldest of flames awoke to the masters' call
An ensemble of beauty was heard throughout the lands
In a cosmic dance of indescribable nature
The time has come and they have returned

Kemet bleeds in the grasp of broken memories
Silence is enthralled by the shouts of golden tears
Now the ancient fear is dying from agonizing pain
For darkness and light have came forth as one
As the reddest of despairs trembles in hidden awe

Once more, from the Duat they came...

Featured in *Kemet - The Year of Revelation*

☥

Book of Sakkara

Tales of the Ancients and Forgotten Spells

"May your flesh be born to life, and may your life encompass more than the life of the stars as they exist."

Pyramid Texts

The artwork presented in the previous page was hand drawn by Tânia Fonseca, depicting an accurate illustration of an Ancient Egyptian relief carving from a stone throne found inside the mortuary temple of Senwosret I[22], representing the legendary struggle between Asetians and Sethians.

✝

T he *Book of Sakkara* is the third and final work that comprises the grimoire manifested as the *Book of Orion*, also known as *Liber Aeternus* in the curriculum of the initiates within the Asetian tradition and to students of the occult venturing through the multilayered path of Asetianism. From all the three major documents it is the only which was not originally written by the author, as its contents originate from some of the most ancient spiritual texts known to mankind.

These texts were translated and compiled according to their magickal and historical significance to the occult student and they are the result of the dedicated work of numerous people, from occultists to Egyptologists, some who are no longer among the living. They are a collection of some of the oldest documented accounts of Ancient Egyptian religious prayers, meditative catalysts, spiritual utterances and metaphysical spells. The particular detail that the Pharaoh Unas, the founder of a pyramid in Sakkara where many of these texts were discovered, was sometimes identified as Orion in his funerary literature provides an even further layer of depth to the mystery and spiritual formulae under scrutiny within this book, presented through the timeless magick of Orion found in the Asetian tradition. The Ancient Egyptian word *Sah*, known for representing the constellation and spiritual concept of Orion, is often omitted from scholarly translations[23]; in some academic cases this is due to being considered an unknown ritualistic orientation, while in other circles it is consciously excluded in light of the nature of its esoteric implications.

The versions presented in this book were translated, assembled and interpreted by members of the Aset Ka in parallel with the study and reference of older public domain works together with the academic theories from Gaston Maspero, Samuel Mercer, Raymond Faulkner, Kurt Sethe and Alexandre Piankoff, whose work in the field

✝

of philological antiquities and Ancient Egyptian language in modern Egyptology has proven to be of invaluable relevance. The majority of the passages were translated in a literal and scientific way from the hieroglyphs presented on the walls and sarcophagi from the pyramids in Sakkara, while in a few cases a proper interpretation was introduced or amends to previous inaccurate translations were applied. It is important to note that this work does not include the full funerary texts ever discovered but only a small sample, and some of the utterances are organized in a specific order and connected in ways that may reveal a certain meaning, while the placement of others is intentionally random, as the finding of order in chaos is one of the necessary accomplishments to any student of the occult.

The nature and language of these ancient religious texts is fascinating, as it has sections of clarity expressed by such straightforward concepts and meanings, while in other excerpts it bears some of the most cryptic, subtle and codified language of all ancient scriptures ever documented. This detail, while brilliant from an occult and literary perspective, can prove daunting and misleading to some students, as the mind must be ready to shift from direct interpretation to a fully meditative and subjective perspective. During the study of the following pages it becomes relevant to keep in mind that we are dealing with very ancient literature and concepts found in Egyptian architecture and funerary objects, so it cannot be approached under a similar light as the magickal texts developed by the author in a contemporary time, like the initiatory utterances found in the *Book of Giza*. A careful observation and integration of *Sigillum 333* into your esoteric practices is highly advised, particularly in times where the light is scarce or the mind is dark.

The awareness and attention to detail that some of these texts can awaken in the initiate makes them a valuable spiritual resource

✝

that, particularly when allowing for the consciousness to commune with the Ba and to drink from the Ka, may enlighten the ways. A few utterances have the power to take you back to important occurrences in history and register those unique moments through an energy and taste that not all will be able to savor. Some can put you back in the mist of battle, others will take you on a quest of pain and sorrow, while a few will allow you to grasp the passion of victory as empires collapse and leaders are forged. Visions and emotions may manifest as you stare at those moments of long gone history, presented in here by the power of the ancient word. It may appear like the small pieces of the greater puzzle can now fit in the tight spots of your own Akashic reality, in order to reveal and liberate nearly forgotten memories of an ancient past. That is the inner alchemy behind these texts and why they should be approached as a spiritual tool in meditation and not just as mere academic literature of an ancient religion and past history. They can tell a tale of events in the Asetian past quite lucidly, in ways that shall never be openly revealed by the Order, presenting a unique source for the seeker to uncover that forgotten truth. But remember, they represent just another simple tool and, as such, these ancient texts are only a device for Understanding. They are merely doors, not the path the initiate must walk when past the gates of those portals. The profound knowledge they can liberate is not found in the words of these texts, but it actually lives within the initiate himself.

Give them a look...
Be ready to be taken on a journey back to the past.

1. May your flesh be born to life, and may your life encompass more than the life of the stars as they exist.

2. She uttered the spell with the magical power of Her mouth.
Her tongue was perfect and it never halted at a word.
Beneficent in command and word was Aset. The one of magical spells.

3. I have been given eternity without limit. Behold, I am the heir of Eternity, to whom have been given everlastingness.

4. You live according to your Will.
You are Wadjet, the Lady of the Flame.
Evil will fall on those who set up against you.

5. Oh Crown of Egypt! Oh Crown great of magic!
Oh fiery Serpent!
Grant that my terror may be as your terror.
Grant that the fear of me be like the fear of you.
Grant that the honor of me be like the honor of you.
Grant that the love of me be like the love of you!
Set my staff at the head of the living.
Set my staff at the head of the spirits.
Grant that my sword prevail over my foes.

☩

Oh Crown!

If you have gone forth from me so have I gone forth from you!

The Great was born in you.

The Serpent has become in you.

The Serpent was born in you.

The Great has adorned you.

As Horus encircled with the protection of his Eye.

6. I have come that I may be your magical protection.

I give breath to your nose, even the north wind that came forth from Atum to your nose.

I have caused that you exist as a God with your enemies having fallen under your sandals.

You have been vindicated in the sky, so that your limbs might be powerful among the Gods.

7. Aset will embrace you in peace.

She will drive away the opponent from your path.

Place your face to the West, that you may illumine the Two Lands.

The dead have stood up to look at you.

Breathing the air and seeing your face.

Like the rising of the Sun-disk in its horizon.

Their hearts are pleased with what you have done.

To you belong eternity and everlastingness.

8. Hail to the waters brought by Shu.

Which the twin springs rose.

In which Geb has bathed his limbs.

So that the hearts lost their fear.

The hearts lost their dread.

He was born in Nun.

Before there was sky.

Before there was earth.

Before there were mountains.

Before there was strife.

Before fear came about through the Eye of Horus!

9. Awake in peace, oh Pure One. In peace.

Awake in peace, Horus from the East. In peace.

Awake in peace, Soul of the East. In peace.

Awake in peace, Horus of the Land. In peace.

You lie down in the boat of night.

You wake up in the boat of day.

For you are he who gazes upon the Gods.

But there is no God who gazes on you!

Oh take him with you.

Alive, to you, oh mother Nut!

Gates of the sky, open for him.

Gates of the Duat, open for him.

He comes to you, make him live!

Order him to sit beside you.

✝

And beside him, who rises in the land!

Lead him to the Goddess beside you.

To make wide the seat at the stairway of the Duat.

Command the Living One, the Son of Sothis, to speak for him.

To establish for him a seat in the sky.

Lead him to the Great Noble.

The beloved of Ptah and his son.

Speak for him. To flourish his urn on Earth.

For he is one with the four nobles:

Imset. Hapi. Duamutef. Qebehsenuf.

Who live by Maat.

Who lean on their staffs.

Who watch over Egypt.

10. You have not died.

You are alive to sit on the throne of Osiris.

The power is in your hand so that you may command the living.

Give the orders to those of the Mysterious Land!

11. For I have looked at you as Horus looked at Aset.

I have looked at you as the Serpent looked at the Scorpion.

I have looked at you as Sobek looked at Neith.

I have looked at you as Seth looked at the Two who are reconciled.

12. There is no God who has become a star without a companion.

Shall I be your companion? Look at me!

You have seen the forms of the children who know their spell.

They are now Imperishable Stars.

May you see the ruler of the Palace: he can only be Horus or Seth.

13. Go after the Sun! You are to purify yourself.

Your bones are those of female hawks, the Goddesses who are in the Duat, so that you may be at the side of the One and leave your realm to your children: your own creation.

Everyone who speaks evil against your name when you rise above is predestined by Geb to be despised within the land and suffer.

You are to purify yourself with the cool water of the stars and you shall strike down upon the ropes of audacity on the arms of Horus.

14. Humanity cries after the Imperishable Stars have carried you.

Enter the place where your creator is united with Geb.

He gives you that which was on the forehead of Horus so that you may become powerful and glorious.

So then you become the one ruling in the West.

15. He has eaten the Red One. He has swallowed the Green One.

The Pharaoh feeds on the lungs of the wise.

His pleasure is to live on hearts as well as on their magic.

☥

16. Your head is that of Horus on the Duat, oh Imperishable One.

Your forehead is the one that has two Eyes, oh Imperishable One.

Your ears belong to the twins of Atum, oh Imperishable One.

Your eyes belong to the twins of Atum, oh Imperishable One.

Your nose is that of a Jackal, oh Imperishable One.

Your teeth are those of Sopedu, oh Imperishable One.

Your arms are those of Hapi and Duamutef.

You need to ascend to the Duat!

As you ascend your legs are those of Imset and Qebehsenuf.

You need to descend to the lower Abyss!

As you descend all your members are those of the twins of Atum.

Oh Imperishable One, you did not die as your Ka cannot die.

You are the Ka!

17. If I live or pass on, I am Osiris.

I enter you and appear through you.

I decay in you and I spring forth from you.

I descend in you and I repose on your side. The Gods are living in me!

As I live and grow in the emmer that sustains the exalted ones.

18. I have come to you, Nephthys.

I have come to you in the evening boat.

I have come to you, truth over the Red.

I have come to you, the one who remembers the Ka.

Remember him!

19. Orion is encircled by the Duat.

When the living horizon purifies itself.

Sothis is encircled by the Duat.

When the living horizon purifies itself.

The Pharaoh is encircled by the Duat.

When the living horizon purifies itself.

He is happy because of them.

He is refreshed because of them.

In the arms of his creator and in the arms of Amon.

20. Hail Atum, who made the sky.

Who created that which exists.

Lord of all that is.

Who gave birth to the Gods.

21. Seth and Nephthys, hurry!

Announce to the Gods of the South and their spirits:

There he comes as an Imperishable Spirit!

If he wills that you shall die, you will die.

If he wills that you shall live, you will live.

22. Geb said and it came forth from the mouth of the Gods:

"Hawk, after you have captured Self you are ensouled and powerful!"

☥

23. The doors of the horizon open and its gates slide.

He has come to you, oh Crown.

He has come to you, Flame Uraeus.

He has come to you, Great One.

He has come to you, Great of Magic.

Purified for you.

In awe before you.

Be pleased with him.

Be pleased with his purification.

Be pleased with the words he says to you

How beautiful is your face when you are pleased.

When you are fresh and young.

A deity has given you birth, the creator of the Gods!

He has come to you, Great of Magic.

It is Horus who fought to protect the Eye, oh Great of Magic.

24. Heka was made for them, to use as a weapon for warding off occurrences. And they created dreams for the night, to see the things of the day.

25. He comes down to meet his adversary and stands up as the greatest chief in his mighty kingdom. Nephthys praised him after he had captured his opponent.

26. You go up and open the ways through the essence of Shu as the embrace of your mother Nut enfolds you. You purify yourself on the horizon and leave that which should be purified from you in the waters of Shu.

27. Let them be in jubilation as the heart of the beast is exalted!
They have swallowed the Eye of Horus in Heliopolis.
The finger of the Pharaoh draws out what is in the navel of Osiris.

28. The Pharaoh is not thirsty.
He is not hungry.
His heart will not faint.
For the arms of the desert keep him away from his hunger.
Fill! Make the hearts full!

29. Judge, arise! Thoth, be high! Sleepers, awake!
The inhabitants of Nubia arise before the great trembler that comes out of the land.

30. The abomination from the Pharaoh is here.
He does not eat the abomination as Seth rejects the poison from the two who crossed the sky.
We call them Horus and Thoth.

31. The Pharaoh was conceived at night.

He was born at night before the morning star.

The Pharaoh was conceived in the watery abyss.

He is being reborn in the watery abyss.

He has come.

He has brought you the nourishment that he found there.

32. A face falls on a face as the face that has seen a face.

The marked knife, black and green, went forth against it.

It has swallowed that which it tasted.

33. Let your two glands of poison remain in the ground!

Let your two rows of ribs be in the cave!

Pour out the liquid!

As the two Kites stand by.

Your mouth is closed by the follower's tool.

The mouth of the follower's tool is closed by the feline.

The tired one is bitten by a serpent.

34. The White Crown should go forth after she has swallowed the Great so that the tongue is not to be seen.

☥

35. The Uraeus is for the Sky.

The snake of Horus is for the Earth.

The cowards imitate Horus.

They have copied the path of Horus.

They know not. They are not knowing.

36. The Serpent of the flame is not to be found in the house of he who possesses Nubt. It is a Serpent that will bite what has slipped into the house of its prey so that it can linger.

37. Horus goes with his Ka.

Seth goes with his Ka.

Thoth goes with his Ka.

The Gods go with his Ka.

The Two Eyes go with his Ka.

You also go with his Ka.

Oh Pharaoh, the arm of your Ka is before you.

Oh Pharaoh, the arm of your Ka is behind you.

Oh Pharaoh, the leg of your Ka is before you.

Oh Pharaoh, the leg of your Ka is behind you.

I give you the Eye of Horus so that your face may be adorned with it.

May the perfume of the Eye of Horus be spread upon you.

38. Osiris, I open your mouth.

The divine metal from the South and the North.

The Eye of Horus that he seeks.

I bring it to you. Put it into your mouth.

Incense from the South and incense from the North.

Take the two Eyes of Horus, the black and the white.

Seize them in front of you so that they can brighten your face.

A white and a black receptacle to be raised up high!

39. May the night be favorable to you.

May the Two Ladies be favorable to you.

A gift that is brought to you is a gift that you can see.

A gift is in front of you. A gift is behind you.

So a gift is your due.

40. Recover the Eye of Horus that was stolen by Seth.

You must rescue it so that he may open your mouth with it.

41. Arise! You who are on the forehead of Horus, arise!

The purest of oils, hurry!

You who are Horus shall be placed on the forehead of the Pharaoh.

You grant him to have power over his body.

You unleash his terror in the eyes of all spirits when they look at him
and of everyone who hears his name.

42. Make the Two Lands bow before this Pharaoh as they bow before Horus! Make the Two Lands fear this Pharaoh as they fear Seth! Be seated before the Pharaoh as a God. Open his path in front of the spirits. That he may stand in front of the dead like Anubis. Forward! Forward, before Osiris!

43. You have caused it to retreat before you.
Sit down! Be silent!
Royal invocation and offering.
The Pharaoh shall take the severed heads of the Followers of Seth.

44. May you open your place in the Duat amongst the stars in the sky!
You are the unique star, the comrade of Hu.
May you look down on Osiris when he gives orders to the spirits.
You stand up high, far from him.
You are not of them as you shall not be of them.

45. Oh Great One who became the sky.
You are strong and you are mighty.
You fill every place with your beauty.
The whole Earth lies beneath you as you possess it!
You embrace the Earth and all things in your arms.
So have you taken this soul in you.
The Indestructible Star within you!

☥

46. See! This Pharaoh stands among you with two horns on his head like two wild bulls. For you are indeed the black ram, son of a black sheep, born of a bright sheep, suckled by four mothers. He comes against you, Horus with watery eyes. Beware of the Horus with red eyes, whose anger is evil, whose powers one cannot withstand! His messengers go. His quick runners run. They announce the one who raised his powers in the East.

47. The fire is laid so the fire shines.

The incense is laid on the fire so the incense shines.

Oh incense, your perfume comes to me.

Oh incense, may my perfume come to you.

Gods, your perfume comes to me.

Gods, may my perfume come to you.

Gods, may I be with you.

Gods, may you be with me.

Gods, may I live with you.

Gods, may you live with me.

Gods, I love you.

Gods, may you love me.

48. They see you as Min who rules over the Two Shrines. He stands behind you. Your brother stands behind you. Your relative stands behind you. You do not go under, you will not be annihilated. Your name remains with men. Your name comes into being with the Gods.

49. The blood of Aset.

The spells of Aset.

The magical powers of Aset.

Shall make this great one strong and shall be an amulet of protection that would do to him the things which he abominates.

50. Your son Horus has crafted this for You. The Great Ones shall tremble when they see the tool that is in Your hand as You come out of the Duat...

51. The Pharaoh has come out of the Island of Fire.

He has revealed Truth in the place of Falsehood.

He is the guardian of cleansing.

The one who watches over the Uraeus on the night of the great flood.

52. The Pharaoh is in control of his Ka.

Uniting the hearts from the one over wisdom.

The great one who is in possession of the Divine Book.

The wisdom at the right of Ra.

53. Oh you who are to be set over the hours. You who shall go in front of Ra. Find a way so that the Pharaoh can pass through the guard of demons with a terrible face!

54. The Pharaoh is on the way to his throne that is in front of the seats behind the God to whom a head has been given back. Adorned with the sharp and strong horn of a beast, he is the one who carries a knife that cuts the throat. This tool is the expeller of pain before the Bull, the one that blesses those in darkness. It is the strong horn of the beast behind the Great Gods. The Pharaoh has overpowered those who were to be punished. He has smashed their heads. The arms of the Pharaoh will not be opposed in the horizon.

55. The two crests of the mountain shall be united.
The two banks of the river will be joined.
The roads will be hidden from the travelers.
The steps will be destroyed for those that go up.
Make tight the rope! Sail the path into the Duat!
Strike the circumference on the realm of Hapi.

56. Ha! Fear and tremble before the storm of the Duat!
He has opened the Earth with that which he knew on the day when he intended to come.

57. One falls down with terror if his ineffable name is spoken.
Not even another God can call him by it.
He, whose name is hidden. Because of this he is a mystery.

58. The praised Serpent is on the throne.

Tefnut, she who supports Shu, has made the seat wide for the Pharaoh in Busiris, Djedet and in the necropolis of Heliopolis.

She erects his two supports in front of the Great Ones.

She excavates a pool for the Pharaoh in the Fields of Time, as she establishes his land in the Fields of Atonement.

The Pharaoh judges in the great flood who is between the Two Opposed Ones.

59. The hearts of his enemies fall before his fingers.

Their intestines are for the inhabitants of the Sky.

Their blood is for those of the Earth.

Their inheritance is to be lost and their homes set on fire.

Their land is to the hunger of the Nile.

60. I am the redness which came forth from Aset.

I am the blood that issued from Nebt-Het.

I am firmly bound up at the waist and there is nothing which the Gods can do for me.

For I am the representative of Ra and I do not die.

61. The horizon inflames before Horus.

The heat of its fiery breath is against you who surrounds the shrine.

Its poisonous heat is against you who wears the Great One.

62. Go away from your seat and lay down on the ground.

If you do not go from your seat the Pharaoh will come with a face like the Great One: the Lord with the head of a lion who became powerful through the injury of his Eye.

Then he will surround you and send a storm against those who did wrong so that it poisons the Primeval Ones.

The Great One rises then in his shrine.

63. Jubilation in the Duat!

The Gods of primeval times saw something new.

Horus was in the sunlight.

The lords of forms serve him as the two whole Enneads turn for him.

He sits on the chair of the Lord of All.

64. Osiris is the Pharaoh in a dust storm.

His horror is on Earth.

The Pharaoh does not enter Geb as he might be destroyed.

He might sleep in his house upon the Earth.

His bones might be broken.

His injuries are removed.

He has purified himself with the Eye of Horus.

His injuries are healed by the two female Kites.

The Pharaoh has freed himself!

65. The abomination of the Pharaoh is to go into darkness so that he does not see.

Upside down.

The Pharaoh comes out in this day and brings Maat with him.

He will not be handed to the Flame of the Gods.

66. The Pharaoh journeys the sky and passes above the Earth.

He kisses the Red Crown as if being cast by a God.

Those in the Three Crowns open their arms to him.

He stands at the East of the vault to the Duat and what rises from the path is brought to him.

He is King, the message of the Storm.

67. He passed by the dangerous place.

The fury of the great lake avoided him.

His charge is not taken by boat.

The shrine of the Gods could not ward him off the road to the stars.

68. He will pass a crossing to the eastern side of the Akhet.

He will pass a crossing to the eastern side of the sky.

His sister is Sothis and the Duat has given him birth.

✝

69. The earth is broken into steps for him towards above.

That he may rise on them towards the Duat.

He rises on the smoke of the great fire.

He flies away as a Scarab on the empty throne that is your boat.

70. Horus takes him to his side.

He purifies him in the lake of the Jackal.

He cleanses his Ka in the lake of the dawn.

When the Two Lands are illuminated he opens the face of the Gods.

He takes his Ka to the Great Temple.

He leads him to the Imperishable Ones.

71. He is a lord of craft whose name even his mother does not know.

He is the one who judges by the side of the One with the hidden name on the day when the Elder is being sacrificed.

Khonsu is his name.

He who slaughters the lords, cuts their throats and takes out what they cary within.

He is the messenger who sends out the punishment.

72. A serpent is coiled by another serpent when a young hippopotamus is entangled.

Earth, swallow that which came out of you!

Monster, lie down and stand away!

The majesty of the bird falls in the water.

Serpent, turn over for Ra may see you!

The head of the great black bull is cut off.

A God in the disguise of a Serpent said to you.

A God-taming Scorpion said to you.

"Turn over, slither into the ground!"

They have said this to you.

73. Thoth is a protector but only when it is dark. Only when it is dark.

74. Hail to you, Daughter of Anubis, who stands at the gates of the sky. You are a friend of Thoth, who stands at the two sides of the ladder. Open the way for our Pharaoh so that he may pass!

75. Your two drops of Poison are on the way to the vessels. Split out the two as they are overfilled with liquid. Allow for the Snake to become kind and the throat of my heart to be saved. Clouds rupture! So that the lion may be drowned in water and the throat of the king be wide.

76. The Cat springs on the neck of the Serpent.

She who brought the Poison.

She strikes on the neck from the holy Serpent.

Who is the one that shall be spared?

✝

77. Ra appears with the Uraeus on his head.

Against this Serpent which comes out of the land.

He cuts off your head with the knife that was in the hand of the Cat.

She who lives in the house of Life.

78. If you love life, oh Horus, upon his life the staff of truth!

Do not lock the gates of the Duat.

Do not seal its doors.

After you have taken his Ka into the Duat.

To the honoring of the Gods. To the friends of the Gods.

Who lean on their staffs.

Guardians of Upper Egypt.

79. There is no word against him on Earth and among men.

There is no crime from him in the Duat and among the Gods.

He has evolved with the word against him.

He has reversed it in order to rise towards the sky.

80. Serene is the sky.

Sothis lives for it is he who is the living son of Sothis.

The two Enneads have purified themselves for him as the Imperishable Stars.

His House that is in the sky will not perish.

His Throne that is on Earth will not be destroyed.

81. The humans hide themselves as the Gods rise above.

Sothis let him fly towards the sky amongst his brothers and the Gods.

Nut the Great has uncovered her arms for him.

82. The doors of the night boat shall not be opened for him.

The doors of the morning boat shall not be opened for him.

His speech should not be judged as that of one in his city.

The doors to the Palace of Annihilation should not be opened for him.

83. The male Serpent is bitten by the female Serpent.

The female Serpent is bitten by the male Serpent.

The Air is enchanted as Earth is enchanted.

Behind, mankind is enchanted.

Enchanted will be the God that is blind.

You, yourself, the Scorpion, will be enchanted.

These are the two knots of Abu that are in the mouth of Osiris.

Knotted for Horus over the Djed.

84. The Pharaoh has taken your necks.

Serve him so that he raises your Ka.

☥

85. Oh you whose back is on his back.

Bring the blood to the offerings that are on the back of Osiris.

So that he may ascend to the Duat.

So that he may serve as Guardian in the sky!

86. I have appeared as Pakhet the Great.

Whose eyes are keen and whose claws are sharp.

The Lioness who sees and catches by night!

87. Infinite time, without beginning and without end.

That is what has been given to me.

I inherit eternity and everlastingness.

Notes

Notes

[1] Authorized King James Bible translation

      Cambridge Edition (1760)

[2] Luis Marques, *Asetian Bible*,

      "Advanced Magick - Planes of Existence" (Aset Ka, 2007)

[3] Dion Fortune, *The Mystical Qabalah*,

      "Binah, the Third Sephirah" (Aquarian Press, 1987)

[4] Lon Milo DuQuette, *Understanding Aleister Crowley's Thoth Tarot*,

      "Secrets of the Rose Cross Back" (Weiser, 2003)

[5] *Sepher Yetzirah*

      Rabbi Isidor Kalisch translation (1877)

[6] Luis Marques, *Asetian Bible*,

      "Sacred Pillars - The Seven Frameworks" (Aset Ka, 2007)

[7] Daniel Chanan Matt, *The Essential Kabbalah: The Heart of Jewish Mysticism*

      (HarperOne, 1996)

[8] Aleister Crowley, *The Book of Thoth: A Short Essay on the Tarot of the Egyptians*,

      The Equinox Vol. III No. V (Weiser, 1974)

[9] Aleister Crowley, *Liber AL vel Legis*, sub figura CCXX as delivered by

      XCIII=418 to DCLXVI (Ordo Templi Orientis, 1938)

[10] Richard H. Wilkinson, *The Complete Gods and Goddesses of Ancient Egypt*

      (Thames & Hudson, 2003)

[11] 江晓原, 历史上的星占学

      (Shanghai Science and Technology Education Press, 1995)

[12] 张闻玉, 古代天文历法讲座

      (Guangxi Normal University Press, 2008)

[13] Luis Marques, *Asetian Bible*,

      "Subtle Anatomy - Shen Centers" (Aset Ka, 2007)

[14] J.R.R. Tolkien, *The Lord of the Rings - The Fellowship of the Ring*,

      "Three is Company" (1954)

[15] Christopher Tolkien and J.R.R. Tolkien, *The Lost Road and Other Writings*,
"The Etymologies" (1987)

[16] James B. Kaler, *Portraits of Stars and their Constellations*
(University of Illinois, 2012)

[17] European Space Agency Hipparcos, *Simbad*
(Centre de Données Astronomiques de Strasbourg, 2012)

[18] John Anthony West, *The Great Work*,
"Initiation One - The Material Plane" (Chance Gardner, 2008)

[19] Luis Marques, *Asetian Bible*,
"The Haunting of the Treacherous Crocodile" (Aset Ka, 2007)

[20] Luis Marques, *Asetian Bible*,
"Watchtowers" (Aset Ka, 2007)

[21] Rosemary Clark, *Sacred Magic Of Ancient Egypt: The Spiritual Practice Restored*
(Llewellyn, 2003)

[22] Mark Lehner, *The Complete Pyramids*,
"The Pyramids at Lisht" (Thames & Hudson 1997)

[23] Richard H. Wilkinson, *The Complete Gods and Goddesses of Ancient Egypt*
(Thames & Hudson, 2003)

✝

The word is sealed.
Em Hotep.

They were only Three.

Yet, they moved a nation.

They were only Seven.

Yet, they conquered the desert.

They became endless.

Yet, they were forgotten.

They became legend.

Then, they were remembered.

Liber Aeternus III.3

CPSIA information can be obtained
at www.ICGtesting.com
Printed in the USA
BVOW04s1930280417
482556BV00001BA/83/P